T5-APQ-687

Language and the *Comedia*

Language and the *Comedia*

Theory and Practice

Catherine Larson

Lewisburg
Bucknell University Press
London and Toronto: Associated University Presses

Associated University Presses
440 Forsgate Drive
Cranbury, NJ 08512

Associated University Presses
25 Sicilian Avenue
London WC1A 2QH, England

Associated University Presses
P.O. Box 39, Clarkson Pstl. Stn.
Mississauga, Ontario
L5J 3X9 Canada

The paper used in this publication meets the requirements of the American National Standard for Permanence of Paper for Printed Library Materials Z39.48-1984.

Library of Congress Cataloging-in-Publication Data

Larson, Catherine, 1950–
Language and the comedia : theory and practice / Catherine Larson.
p. cm.
Includes bibliographical references (p.) and index.
ISBN 0-8387-5180-6 (alk. paper)
1. Spanish drama—Classical period, 1500–1700—History and criticism. 2. Spanish drama—Classical period, 1500–1700—History and criticism—Theory, etc. 3. Spanish language—Classical period, 1500–1700—Style. I. Title.
PQ6105.L37 1991
862′.309—dc20 89-46406
CIP

PRINTED IN THE UNITED STATES OF AMERICA

For George Ann and Sidney

Contents

Acknowledgments

I owe a debt of gratitude to a number of people who have given me help and support in completing this project. Special recognition goes to seven colleagues and friends who helped me immeasurably: to Danny Anderson, William R. Blue, Charles Ganelin, James Mandrell, Kathleen Myers, Elias L. Rivers, and Robert C. Spires I extend my thanks.

I would also like to thank the editors and publishers who graciously allowed me to reprint three of the article-length studies that appear in amended form in this volume: Thomas Lathrop (for the study of *La dama boba,* which first appeared in *Things Done with Words: Speech Acts in Hispanic Drama,* edited by Elias L. Rivers), Andrew Bush (for the study of *La verdad sospechosa,* found in the *Revista de estudios hispánicos*), and Bucknell University Press (for the chapter on *La dama duende,* forthcoming in a volume of essays titled *The Perception of Women in Spanish Theater of the Golden Age,* edited by Anita K. Stoll and Dawn L. Smith). In the first two cases, the articles have been substantively and substantially revised since their original publication; in the case of the study of *La dama duende,* minimal changes have been made. I would further like to thank Arturo Pérez Pisonero for allowing me to include within this study the part of the chapter on *Cada uno para sí* that appeared in *Texto y espectáculo: Nuevas dimensiones críticas de la comedia.*

Finally, I am grateful to Indiana University, which gave me the summer faculty fellowship that allowed me to finish this project in a timely manner by funding my research at the Biblioteca Nacional in Madrid, as well as the grant that funded the translation of the Spanish quotations. In that regard, I owe a special debt of thanks to Baltasar Fra Molinero for his sensitive translations.

Language and the *Comedia*

Introduction: Language and the *Comedia*

It could be stated fairly that in the past twenty years, *comedia* scholars (that is, those engaged in studying Spanish Golden Age drama) have been reluctant to experiment with contemporary theory and interpretation, some elements of which are already becoming passé for a number of French and Anglo-American literary critics.[1] Recently, however, *comedia* critics—along with other scholars of Hispanic literature—have begun to explore a seemingly endless number of ways of viewing texts. With the advent of poststructuralist theory and criticism, the literary text came to be perceived as something other than a historical artifact or logocentric unit. J. Hillis Miller's description of the phenomenon is particularly apt:

> A distinctive feature of English and American literary criticism today is its progressive naturalization, appropriation, or accommodation of recent continental criticism. . . . The "new turn" in criticism, which is a return of the old, is characterized by a focus on language as the central problematic of literary study. This focus determines a breaking down of barriers and a putting into question of grounds, even of the apparently solid basis of new linguistic theory. This rediscovery of an often hidden center of gravity in literature might be called the linguistic moment. . . . The new turn in criticism involves an interrogation of the notion of the self-enclosed literary work and of the idea that any work has a fixed, identifiable meaning. The literary work is seen in various ways as open and unpredictably productive. ("Stevens' Rock" 332–33)

Each in its own way, New Criticism, structuralism, and poststructuralism led to a focus on—and an interest in—language, although each was also different from the ongoing tradition of philological approaches to literature and to language that had characterized literary studies in the first half of the century. Deconstructive criticism raised new questions regarding the determinacy of language and any kind of consequent faith in the power of the word to reflect—much less, create—reality. Within the newly defined parameters of the historical context, Marxist and feminist readings proffered alternative methods of viewing language in its relationship to society and, consequently, to such social products as literary texts.

This study proposes to show how a focus on language, which is manifest in many of the recent trends in literary theory, can help to open some of the canonical texts of Golden Age theater to new readings. This approach is certainly not fundamentally radical. Indeed, the seminal studies of the *comedia* in the twentieth century have hardly ignored the importance of the discourse found in Golden Age texts. Yet a number of the analytical methods and theories introduced in the past thirty years can suggest something new to teachers and students of the *comedia.* First, those recent trends supply a more specific and detailed vocabulary for dealing with our earlier intuitions and assumptions regarding the role of language in the dramatic text. In addition, as William Cain explains, "Theory exposes errors in what has been done in the past, highlights mistakes and unexamined assumptions in what is being done in the present, and remains skeptical, if also hopeful, about alternatives for the future" ("Reply to Lentricchia's 'On Behalf of Theory'" 221). Finally, theory can often offer a context, a way of viewing the text that, to cite Josué Harari, allows "what was *always already* inscribed in its texture to resurface" ("Critical Factions/ Critical Fictions" 37).

Since this book is meant to be practical rather than purely theoretical, theory's role in analysis must be addressed, if only briefly, before moving to the specific ways it can suggest new readings for old plays.[2] Austin Quigley offers one perspective:

> What we have long conceived of as literary theory has taken many forms, but it has constantly sought to locate the appropriate relationship between general principles and particular cases. . . . Literary theory can suitably multiply the armory of instruments: it can invite us to appropriate the most advanced forms of thinking in related fields such as psychology, sociology, philosophy, linguistics, and anthropology. ("Wittgenstein's Philosophizing" 227, 230)

Steven Knapp and Walter Benn Michaels offer a useful synthesis of the function of literary theory, although both critics could certainly be said to represent the ranks of those who oppose much of its use in contemporary interpretative practice:

> Theory attempts to solve—or to celebrate the impossibility of solving—a set of familiar problems: the function of authorial intention, the status of literary language, the role of interpretive assumptions, and so on. ("Against Theory" 723)

All of these observations form part of the exploration of theory that orients the approach in this study. The best explanation of all, though, might well be Stanley Fish's simple question, "isn't the very point of theory to throw light on or reform or guide practice?" ("Consequences" 106). This book presents theory as a means of helping to achieve a new level of understanding of certain aspects of the primary texts that are analyzed; the insights gleaned from a number of contemporary theoretical models will guide interpretive practice.

Several points, however, must be borne in mind. First, in every case, the theoretical models used to structure those readings should never be viewed as ends in and of themselves. They may offer tools for approaching the dramatic text from a different perspective, but they do not constitute any kind of absolute methodology for analyzing the theater in general or a specific text in particular. Rather, these models can allow us to see and to articulate more clearly aspects of the texts that were always a part of their make-up. The primacy of the dramatic text is regarded as a given in this study, and the theories used are intended to work in partnership with the dramatic texts as part of the development of the reading.

Second, the readings of the plays treated here are, in the best sense of the word, incomplete. They do not pretend to examine every aspect of the plays in question, but rather, they explore certain key elements of those plays from distinct perspectives, raising questions and discussing issues that may well apply to other parts of the same text or even to texts from other genres or epochs. Moreover, the variety of dramas and dramatists examined is intended to parallel the open nature of the various approaches utilized in the readings. The methodologies themselves are unresolved and, therefore, incomplete. John Ellis explains:

> any new theoretical position, in whatever field of inquiry, has always been and will always be subject to debate between its advocates and its critics, and in the course of that debate will almost certainly be revised, redefined, characterized more sharply, and eventually either generally accepted or dropped and forgotten. ("What Does Deconstruction" 259)

What this means if that since the theories themselves are still part of an evolutionary process, so, too, are the readings proposed in this critical enterprise. These studies of language in the *comedia* are intended to suggest the vast possibilities inherent in the approaches used—in their general applicability, and in their usefulness on a number of levels and for a wide variety of audiences. In addition, since a reader's horizons of experience and expectations change with the passage of time, each successive reading of the primary text is part of a historically evolving process.[3] Consequently, every reading is, by definition, old, new, and at the same time, incomplete.

Further, the ways that the plays are examined in this book are intended to complement, rather than to supplant, the kinds of historical, thematic, and performance-oriented responses to the texts that define the critical heritage of each of those dramas. It is, therefore, essential to remember that these plays were written to be performed onstage for an audience temporally and geographically removed from the times and places in which the linguists, critics, and philosophers who developed the theoretical models explored here wrote and lived. The union of theory and practice, however, need not threaten such realities. As we explore the manner in which language functions in a number of *comedia* texts, we must bear in mind the climate of their creation, the viability of their staging, and the fundamental link between text and spectacle that characterizes the theater.

It is, therefore, useful to reconsider the distinct aspects of the texts that are treated here. Keir Elam reminds us to contemplate two texts when we study the theater: the written text and the text of the performance ("Language" 140).[4] In dealing with plays, the critic should remain cognizant of the dual nature of the text and the relationships between language and each of these two levels.

The new readings found in this book investigate the relationship between dramatic language and the levels of communication set up within the text, as well as between the text, its author, and the reader/spectator. As noted above, these two levels always exist in the theater: communication on the mimetic level (that of the microtext)[5] and the two-pronged level of creation-of-text (dramatist-text) and reception-of-text (reader/spectator-text). This last level corresponds to Jakobson's communicative model (that of sender-message-receiver), with the notable exception of the extra filters operant in theatrical communication. Directors' and actors' interpretations intervene between authorial production and audience reception; moreover, an audience member viewing a theatrical production always—and necessarily—witnesses a unique performance. Audience response (the influence of members of the audience on other audience members and on the actors), the actors' changing performances each night, the physical situation (ranging from the existence of such elements as a creative staging of the play to physical problems—faulty lighting or inclement weather), the knowledge that each performance can never be exactly duplicated—all of these factors combine to express the unique type of communication that is so typical of the theater. In addition, as Elizabeth Burns notes in *Theatricality:*

> Unlike all other forms of literary art a play is remade every time it is performed. The remaking occurs through the performance in which dramatists, producer, actors and audience all participate. (23)

Now, it could be argued that each new reading of *any* literary text (be it a play, a poem, or a novel) remakes that text in a particular way, but the theater does tender a very special kind of remaking. A play involves more participants and is filtered through more levels, all of which can affect (in geometric permutations) the other factors involved.

Yet, without disregarding for one moment the imperative of viewing the text as a potential performance text, it is also both fair and fitting to insist on the central role of the written text in the theater and, more specifically, in Golden Age theater. Performance, at least of the *comedia,* cannot begin without a written text. Any analysis of dialogue, of linguistic interaction, must consequently recognize the primacy of the script in its written form: it is both the text and the pre-text for performance. As a result, I have tried throughout the book to bear in mind the complexity of the semiotic process inherent in the performance text, although my primary focus is on the object that constitutes the written text. The distance between seventeenth-century staging practices and late twentieth-century understanding of them mandates, at least to a certain extent, this interest in the words contained in the written text. More importantly, however, while we must always posit the representational aspect of every play text that we analyze—and while we must further acknowledge how language unites with other modes of signifying (such as gesture)[6]—in the theater, discourse holds a unique position, which is due, in part, to the factors that distinguish it from more "ordinary" conversation. As Elam observes, the fact that language in the theater is one part of a general semiotic process does not mean:

> that it suffers from any actual or absolute loss of power (for example, rhetorical power). On the contrary, language in the theater is generally far more "powerful" rhetorically and otherwise, than in its social usage. ("Language" 147)

This is particularly true of the *comedia,* whose composition in verse obliges us to consider language as a key element of its creation and calls our attention to the union of poetry and theater that is inherent in Golden Age drama.[7]

Although the plays analyzed in this book will be approached from a variety of theoretical angles, the constant will be an emphasis on dramatic communication. Speech act theory, Wittgenstein's theory of the language game, semiotics (with implications for a feminist reading of a dramatic text), deconstruction, and reception theory will all be utilized as tools for exploring the communicative relationships existing among the dramatist, the text, and the audience, as well as between and among the characters within the play.

It is important to note, however, that the interpretive applications of these theories to specific texts were not undertaken at random; all theoretical models do not help to unlock all literary texts. In other words, some theories serve as more effective elucidating tools for analyzing specific types of plays than others. There is no question but that a major problem in past applications of many of these models is that some critics have tried to make the texts fit the theories. Such efforts are frequently doomed to failure because they force a reading on the literary text that either cannot be sustained by textual evidence or that expands the theory beyond reasonable bounds.

On the other hand, a firm grounding in a number of contemporary approaches to literature gives the critic something to work with. As each primary text is read and reread, the critic can search for a useful way to approach that reading. How does a critic forge a match between primary texts and elucidating theories? On a most basic level, by joining his or her theoretical repertoire with a solid critical repertoire (knowledge of the seminal readings of the play, the period, the dramatist, and the genre) and with a close reading of the text, and by exploring interpretive possibilities as well as discarding some models as unworkable, the critic eventually narrows the field to include only those methods that help render that specific text intelligible.

John S. Brushwood uses a similar type of approach in his theoretical analyses of several nineteenth-century Latin American novels. Consequently, he has dealt with many of the same issues I confronted in my own attempt to reconcile theory and practice:

> There is variety in literary texts and also in analytical procedures, and it is tempting to think that within this variety ideal associations exist. It is doubtful, however, that there is a perfect analytical procedure for a given text. On the other hand, one may reasonably assume that some particular critical approach can best illuminate a certain aspect of a given work or answer a specific question raised by the critic. . . . The critical approach used for each novel was selected because it promised to answer a question that interested me with respect to the meaning of the text. (*Genteel Barbarism* ix)

Brushwood's comments underscore the approach I have tried to follow in this book. My goal is to show how a number of theories can help to illustrate or heighten certain aspects of these dramatic texts. The texts serve as representative examples of Golden Age drama, although it is clear that some specific categories (the *comedia de santos* [saints' plays], the *auto sacramental* [sacramental plays]) were not used in the analyses. The only implications that should be drawn from this fact are that time and space constraints affected my selections and that frequently the examples of linguistic self-reflexivity found in the comic works made them particularly interesting objects of investigation. In each chapter, however, the plays and corresponding theories were chosen because they called attention to a specific type of communicative problem or relationship. Sometimes a single theoretical concept helped to inform my reading of a particular drama; often a number of ideas worked in concert to shape the way I came to view the text: contemporary linguistic and literary theories frequently exist in a symbiotic relationship. In all cases, however, I tried to design the theoretical aspects of the readings so that they would strengthen the textual explications without overpowering them. The book is less a history of contemporary literary theory than a practical guide, a means of exploring from a different perspective the making of meaning.

A final issue at hand in the union of theory and practice concerns the critic's view of the text that will be examined. Although the ideas that language is indeterminate and that the text is unrecuperable inform much of poststructuralist thought, the interpretive models used in this book posit the belief that literary theory can help unravel some of the mysteries that lie within the *comedia* texts that are analyzed. Bruce W. Wardropper suggests that:

> The successful application to Spanish literature of theories and techniques developed since the heyday of New Criticism has been possible only because [scholars] . . . have believed in the determinacy and referentiality of the texts they were studying. ("An Apology for Philology" 179)

I would argue that these texts be viewed not as determinate products but as processes. Interpretation can, I believe, only function successfully if we trust in the possibility that we can find new readings of the texts we study, ones that allow us to link the past with the present. Although we cannot recover completely the text's existence in the moment of its creation, we nevertheless can attempt to encounter new tools for increasing our understanding of the object we hold in our hands. This does not negate the impact of the reader and his or her response to that literary object. On the contrary, it suggests the possibility of revising the ways we place the text within a synchronic frame or examine it as part of a diachronic trajectory.

The book treats seven different plays, each from a distinct theoretical perspective. The first three chapters use different aspects of the general linguistic/philosophical approach called speech act theory as their point of departure. The study of *La dama boba* [*The Lady Simpleton*] reveals Félix Lope de Vega's insistence upon the importance of language and the interplay of varying levels of metadiscourse in the comedy. The second chapter shows how a typical late Golden Age comedy (represented here by Francisco Rojas Zorrilla's *Entre bobos anda el juego* [*All the Players Were Fools*]) relies upon linguistic misfiring and games-playing, which may be further elucidated via the notion of the Cooperative Principle developed by H. Paul Grice. The third chapter deals with the relationship between naming and characterization in Juan Ruiz de Alarcón's *La verdad sospechosa* [*The Suspect Truth*], in which the conventional relationship between sign and referent is frequently subverted. The fourth chapter uses a different kind of linguistic approach: Keir Elam's appropriation of Wittgenstein's concept of the language game. The five categories that Elam has explored in his study of Shakespeare are related in this chapter to Lope's *El caballero de Olmedo* [*The Knight from Olmedo*]. The approach of the fifth chapter could be labeled feminist, but it also rests on a firm grounding in semiotics. Pedro Calderón de la Barca's *La dama duende* [*The Spirit Lady*] is presented as a study of simultaneously conflicting signifiers that illuminate the dramatist's presentation of his protagonist as both the archetypical "angel in the house" and as a kind of demon. The sixth textual analysis, a deconstructive reading of a central issue in Lope's *Fuenteovejuna* [*The Sheep Well*], points toward a new direction in terms of the theoretical approaches found in this book. This chapter is a multiple deconstruction in that it reveals an attitude toward language that is, in many ways, completely at odds with the linguistic perspective seen up to that point in the chapters that have their bases in less nihilistic approaches. My study of *Fuenteovejuna* is intended to suggest the openness and the methodological possibilities of the theoretical models explored here, and as such, it really is much less at odds with the overall tone of the book than a first glance might suggest. Finally, the relationship between the dramatist and his text and between reading and writing is the focus of the last chapter, which uses the work of Hans Robert Jauss as its theoretical base. This last chapter represents a rather extreme example of the union of theory and practice, since rather than attempting to apply the theoretical model directly, it utilizes Jauss's ideas as a metaphor for examining Calderón's *Cada uno para sí* [*Every Man for Himself*]. Plot summaries of each of these plays are provided in an appendix.[8]

As noted above, the textual analyses found in this book range in type from close readings of the character-to-character level of communication to an exploration of the communication that occurs between and among the author, the text, and the audience. That diversity of approaches to theatrical communication reflects not only the complex nature of theatrical communication, but also shows how a focus on language can extend to each level of the communicative hierarchy, as well as how pragmatics (language in use) allows for the union of theory and practice in the creation of usable—and useful—interpretive models.

1
Language as Subject and Object of Lope's *La dama boba*

What I shall have to say here is neither difficult nor contentious; the only merit I should like to claim for it is that of being true, at least in parts.
—J. L. Austin

Our examination of language in the *comedia* begins on a thematic level with an analysis of a typical Lope de Vega comedy serving to indicate the degree to which this Golden Age dramatist self-consciously recognized the power of words. The emphasis here is on the transforming power of the dramatic discourse of the play—not in the literal sense that all writers use words, but rather in the ways that Lope's two female characters (and, particularly, his protagonist, Finea) employ language to create new realities. In their use of language, they transcend the conventionalized limits that words possess for their listeners in order to develop alternative modes of expression, modes that will enable them to achieve a controlling position from which to confront their world. Linguistic control, as we will see, can foster situational control for these female characters, who would otherwise be trapped in the patriarchal world of the *comedia.* Language, then, functions as both the subject and object of *La dama boba* [*The Lady Simpleton*], a comedy that helps to clarify the types of linguistic self-awareness that inform so many *comedia* texts.

In *Shakespeare's Universe of Discourse: Language-Games in the Comedies,* Keir Elam discusses the historical reasons for the linguistic self-consciousness found in Shakespeare's comedies:

> Shakespeare's was an age in which language occupied a central place in all areas of cultural endeavour and of socio-political conflict: in religious controversy (e.g. the dispute over "sacred" verbal formulae that underlay the Reformation); in geographical exploration (the contact with unknown tongues); in philosophical debate (e.g. the competing Aristotelian and Platonic conceptions of the linguistic sign); in the

> politics of education (the benefits or otherwise of instruction in rhetoric); in the new science (the reliability of language as a cognitive tool); in the new national consciousness (the affirmation of the vernacular) and of course in the arts, not least in the theatre itself (the debate on the morality of plays and their discourse). There can be no question that the intense linguistic consciousness of the Elizabethan period influenced in turn the very linguistic make-up of the Elizabethan drama, not only in its rhetorical complexity but in its very concern with language in its manifold aspects. (1–2)

Elam's points regarding this historical interest in language are equally relevant to an analysis of the *comedia,* since many of the factors discussed above with reference to Shakespeare underscore the types of linguistic awareness seen in Spanish Golden Age dramatic texts as well.[1] The Golden Age was also "an age in which language occupied a central place," both on a cultural and sociopolitical plane. The world that *comedia* texts explored was made real through language, but language itself often assumed a new role of its own. In this new context dialogue was not only a principal medium for transmitting the dramatist's ideas to the audience, but also often became the subject of the play itself. Again, Elam explains:

> in an age that elects language as both primary channel and primary target for its enthusiasms, for its suspicions, and even for its wars, the dramatic and theatrical potential of verbal events in themselves becomes virtually limitless. (*Shakespeare's Universe* 2)

The study of such verbal events has evolved considerably in the twentieth century. J. L. Austin's lectures in the late 1950s (later collected and published under the title *How to Do Things with Words*) represent a milestone in twentieth-century literary theory. Research in the field has proliferated since Austin's pioneering work; speech act theory has experienced a surge of interest from both language philosophers and literary critics. In the former group, John R. Searle and H. Paul Grice stand as representatives of those who have revised a number of Austin's ideas in linguistically oriented studies. In the latter group, critics such as Richard Ohmann, Mary Louise Pratt, and Stanley Fish have used speech act theory in literary analysis. In recent years, the theory has served as an elucidating model for texts ranging from Shakespeare's plays to *Mary Hartman, Mary Hartman.*[2]

What is a speech act theory of literature? The answer is that there are many theories, and there is none. This is partially true because even early in *How to Do Things with Words,* Austin showed that he regarded the theory as an evolving model. His text moves from a belief in the existence of two types of utterances—performatives (in which "the issuing of the utterance is the performing of an action" [Austin, *How to Do* 6]) and constatives (true-false statements that describe or report)—to the rejection of that idea in favor of a theory that posited three main types of speech acts (locutionary, illocutionary, and perlocutionary). Mary Louise Pratt and Elizabeth Traugott explain the first two types of acts:

> As its name suggests, speech act theory treats an utterance as an act performed by a speaker in a context with respect to an addressee. Performing a speech act involves performing (1) A *locutionary act,* the act of producing a recognizable grammatical utterance in the language, and (2) an *illocutionary act,* the attempt to accomplish some communicative purpose. Promising, warning, greeting, reminding, informing, and commanding are all distinct illuctionary acts. (*Linguistics for Students of Literature* 229)

Perlocutions have to do with producing effects. Consequently, if I warn you (an illocutionary act), I may also alert or alarm you (Austin, *How to Do* 118–21). The core of this theory is a focus on the kinds of transactions that take place between interlocutors. Consequently, the idea of "doing things with words," the heart of Austin's philosophy, would seem particularly applicable to the study of literature and especially to the analysis of a performance-oriented medium such as the theater. Austin's insights on the nature of discourse can "make explicit the internal workings of a text . . . these approaches give a new perspective on a central concern of literary theory, namely, the relations between reader, author, and text" (Pratt and Traugott, *Linguistics* 255).

The limits of speech act theory were expanded with each subsequent revision of Austin and with each new literary application of the model, which survives today as a general approach that combines elements of linguistics and philosophy for the stylistic analysis of literary communication, as well as the analysis of naturally occurring dialogue. Speech act theory offers the most tantalizing promise to literary scholars when it serves as a means of stimulating new insights and opening texts that might have been thought exhausted by critical explication, and enables us to see those texts with a fresh eye. As a result, Austin's type of discourse study can lead us to reexamine and reevaluate not only the specific texts that interest us, but the entire role of language in drama.

The analysis of the language in a play can take many forms and have many functions. Although on a fundamental level any critical analysis deals with language, the means of approaching that language have varied in different epochs. An interest in poetic language lies at the heart of a stylistic approach to versification or imagery patterns; studies of the speech of different types of characters (including the comic buffoon, the *gracioso,* or those who use *sayagués*)[3] illustrate yet another way to use linguistic models in literary interpretation. Certainly any discussion of characterization and theme uses language as the basis of its approach. What, then, does speech act theory add to literary analysis?

Most obviously it offers an organized, taxonomic vocabulary for discussing a number of different issues and ideas, some of which might only have been intuited previously. The analysis of dramatic discourse, one possible use of speech act theory, complements the studies of naturally occurring dialogue or everyday conversation.[4] In addition, by its very name, speech act theory points to the union of speech and action that *is* drama. It even goes a step further by underscoring the fact that when we—or, in this case, the characters in a play—*speak,* we also *act,* and every example of dialogue represents not merely the production of an utterance, but also an intention on the part of the speaker, the goal of which is to produce some sort of response in the listener.

Further, because speech act theory stresses the interaction between speakers and listeners, a critic can use it to examine questions of linguistic competence and to explore in a detailed and coherent manner the importance of contextual overtones. M. H. Short discusses the advantages of this type of approach for analyzing dramatic discourse:

> in play texts the variable of situational context is more closely controlled and hence more amenable to examination. Similarly, in drama notions like cooperation, seriousness and so on, which are implicit in everyday conversation, are often explicitly negotiated by the characters or demonstrated by the playwright. ("Discourse Analysis" 200)

Speech act theory can underscore the dramatist's use of distinct types of vocabulary, self-conscious language, or performative verbs (Austin's examples of verbs that *do* as well as *say*) in key roles, contrasts between written and oral discourse, or patterns of linguistic behavior that emerge as motifs within the text. It can also expose who has the control, power, or authority in a typical dramatic situation; it can reveal examples of subversion occurring on a linguistic level; and it can relate these issues to the large and small conflicts that occur in the plays that are analyzed.[5]

Consequently, the social conventions that were so important in the Golden Age and in the *comedia* can be explored in a meaningful way with this type of approach. We may question how these conventions are made comprehensible and how they are either undercut or upheld in dramatic texts. Moreover, we can see *how* linguistic conventions function and how they are tied to other social conventions, such as the honor code, gender roles, social hierarchies, etc.[6]

We can therefore study the ways in which characters violate the implicit rules and conventions[7] that govern dramatic discourse, for example, the moments when a character tells lies or refuses to speak (silence often being even more powerful than speech), when there is a conflict between two truths (a kind of linguistic double bind), when a character deceives with the truth, or even when a character encounters the consequences of linguistic deferral, as in the famous words of Don Juan Tenorio, "Tan largo me lo fiáis" [There's plenty of time to pay my dues]. Finally, we can examine the links between language and convention by analyzing scenes in which characters foreground language: when they appear to be conscious of their own discourse, when they comment upon the process of speaking or the impossibility of communicating effectively, and when they play their roles in a (linguistically) self-conscious manner, at times even transforming themselves into the "directors" of the actions of other characters. These last cases lie at the heart of the following analysis, which stresses how, in a very real sense, language serves as both the subject and object of *La dama boba*.

We will see that as the principal characters in *La dama boba* grapple with their awakening to love and their consequent inner strife, their thoughts turn to language itself—to language as the only means at their disposal to make sense of, to control, themselves and their situation, to language as a frustratingly inadequate tool for expressing the unexpressable. In this play, as in so many others, Lope was able to articulate the connections between language and comedy, a textual strategy that Melveena McKendrick explores in her analysis of *El castigo sin venganza* [*Punishment Without Revenge*]:

> The play seems . . . to reveal clearly that Lope, long before the advent of linguistic theory and philosophy, was aware of the creative and

manipulative functions of language and aware, too, that non-truth and less-than-truth is a primary part of this function. Language has an infinite capacity to misinform, conceal, invent, leave ambiguous, and mislead. . . . The main function of speech is rarely that of straightforward communication, and Lope knew it. ("Language and Silence" 83)

Language in *La dama boba* functions in much the same way. The play continually underscores linguistic manipulation—both in its ordinary, "everyday" use as dialogue and in its metaliterary and extratextual references. Words are employed quite differently by the two sisters, Finea and Nise. Throughout much of the play, Finea is presented as a dunce who cannot understand the relationship between words and reality; she contrasts vividly with her well-educated and highly sophisticated sibling. The sisters' two principal suitors, Liseo and Laurencio, also presented as opposing characters, differ dramatically in their reactions to Finea's boorish behavior. Lope reveals the dualities seen in these two sets of characters through their use and abuse of language, for in *La dama boba* words make the man or woman. What finally happens to these characters is more a function of what they say and how they say it than of what they do or how they do it. Language—or, even more specifically, language *as* action[8]—becomes the ultimate determinant of each character's fate.

Two lines of dialogue illustrate beautifully this relationship between dialogue, plot, and theme. As she tries desperately to control the course of the dramatic action, Nise, the linguistically adept sister, cries, "Yo quiero hablar claro" [I want to speak clearly]. Her formerly simple sibling, Finea, describes her own transformation in linguistic terms, telling her lover, "Por hablarte supe hablar" [By talking to you, I learned how to speak]. These examples of Lope's interest in language and in communication are merely representative of the large number of self-conscious references to language found in *La dama boba;* a close examination of these linguistically oriented elements suggests a self-referential substructure for the play, in which the power of language to constitute reality becomes the focus of attention.

A linguistically oriented approach to this play is hardly revolutionary; indeed, this one offers a reading that complements earlier interpretations of the comedy. Critical attention with respect to *La dama boba* has traditionally centered upon its rich imagery, its underlying philosophical bases, and its strength as a comic work.[9] All these studies have attested to the play's success through the years and to its validity as a powerful work of art. As James

Holloway affirms, *La dama boba* reflects "Lope's view of reality given form in poetry, in action, in characterization" ("Lope's Neoplatonism: *La dama boba*" 239). Yet, as noted above, the play operates on another level, as well. It is a dramatic text that foregrounds language. It not only deals with language in the ways that all plays deal with language, but it self-consciously calls attention to itself as drama and as linguistically constructed art.[10] An exploration of these self-conscious attempts to communicate can thus expose the play's underlying structure and its underlying message for the reader/spectator.

To understand how language becomes the determining factor in the play's resolution, we must understand how the two sisters' use of language is turned upside down in the course of *La dama boba*. Nise, intelligent, although at times both arrogant and pedantic, presents herself as an authority on literature. As literary critic, she comments upon drama, prose, and poetry, even to the point of alluding to a certain Lope de Vega. Yet, by discussing the act of literary creation within the world of another literary work—within the dramatic text—Nise constantly reminds us of the intimate relationship between language and art. Her literary lectures thus subtly illuminate the role of language in constituting and transforming reality, serving as self-conscious reminders that words are the media that writers use to create dramatic texts. Keir Elam notes, "In the drama, the metalinguistic function often has the effect of foregrounding language as object or event by bringing it explicitly to the audience's attention" (*Semiotics* 156). When characters in a dramatic text talk about literature, and when words remind us about how language functions, we begin to center on the relationship between language and literary creation. Nise's self-conscious use of language, her metacritiques of fictional texts, bring (dramatic, fictional, poetic) language to the audience's attention and point to the relationship between writers, texts, and readers.

Nise, however, also often fails to take her own listeners into account; she talks down to them, especially when her authority is challenged. She thus emerges as a character who abuses the conventions—the rules of discourse—that govern communication. A key example of this aspect of Nise's characterization is the scene in which she meets with several suitors in a literary "academy," discussing literature and critiquing one of the men's original sonnets. The sonnet functions in much the same way as other literary texts that are embedded in the play, displaying language by illuminating the ways that words transform reality in artistic creations.[11]

Here, however, the literary creation falls on its face—at least for Nise. Nise claims that the sonnet is unclear, obscure, and affected. She exclaims, "Ni una palabra entendí" [I didn't understand a word of it] (1.7.539).

Although the poet, Duardo, explicates his poem for her, Nise remains arrogantly and adamantly critical: "No discurras, por tu vida; / vete a escuelas" [Don't explain, for crying out loud; / go back to grammar school] (1.7.575–76). Nise, the pseudointellectual, has failed to comprehend fully the manipulation of artistic language by another "intellectual"; she remains convinced that Duardo is incapable of using poetic language effectively. In this early part of the play, Nise maintains her own pretentious manipulation of language and literary criticism, but she gradually becomes less sure of herself as the comedy progresses and as she is supplanted in the role of linguistic mistress by her sister, Finea.

Finea, the *dama boba,* begins the play as a total simpleton. Ronald Surtz explains her linguistic role: "In the verbal world of the *comedia, bobería* [stupidity] is manifested above all as a failure to grasp symbolic language. Finea interprets literally words and expressions that are used in a figurative sense" (163). Her understanding of how language functions is thus ingenuous in the extreme. Finea's language patterns are illuminated in her school lesson on the alphabet:

Rufino. Di aquí: *b, a, n: ban.*
Finea. ¿Dónde van?
¿Que se van, no me decías?
Rufino. Letras son; ¡míralas bien!
Finea. Ya miro.
Rufino. *B, e, n: ben.*
Finea. ¿Adónde?
Rufino. ¡Adonde en mis días
no te vuelva más a ver!
Finea. ¿Ven, no me dices? Pues ya voy.

[*Rufino.* Repeat after me: *g, o: go.* / *Finea.* Where are they going? Didn't you tell me they're going? / *Rufino.* They are letters of the alphabet; look at them! / *Finea.* I'm looking. / *Rufino. c, o, m, e: come.* / *Finea.* Where to? / *Rufino.* Someplace where I'll never see you again! / *Finea.* But didn't you tell me to come? Well, I'm going.]
(1.6.336–46)

This speech offeres a striking example of how dramatic language can be used for characterization. It also utilizes language as its own referent. By presenting a lesson on words, the scene foregrounds language as object, accentuating the theme of learning language—be it the alphabet, everyday discourse, or the language of love—and tying the use of words to the central themes of the play. Finea's self-referential lesson on the alphabet focuses our attention on the act of learning; this concept will resurface later in the play when Finea learns not only how to spell, but to love, to use language efficaciously, and to become the mistress of her own fate.

We may then connect Finea's school lesson to the play as a whole and to the relationship between the play and the reader/spectator. Although the other characters onstage react negatively to her linguistic naïveté, Finea's failures to understand and to communicate are wholly felicitous for the audience.[12] We are simultaneously able to laugh at her linguistic misfirings and to see how language affects and effects characterization, while we are subtly reminded of the important role that words assume throughout the play. Lope indicates here that language is, in part, what the play is about; ironically, he does so by humorously displaying the potential of language to create *and* to obfuscate.

We also see that the early contrasting portraits of the two sisters are based on only one thing: linguistic competence. For completely antithetical reasons, neither sister is successful in the art of communication. Their father therefore summarizes the need for a middle ground between the two extremes:

> pues la virtud es bien que el medio siga:
> que Finea supiera más que sabe,
> y Nise menos.

> [For virtue should always seek the middle ground: / Finea should know more than she does, / and Nise less.]
>
> (1.3.238–40)

At this point in the play, Lope has already begun to prepare us for the transformations that will take place. By means of the emphasis that he gives to words and to their creative and transforming power, the dramatist opens the door to the changes that will soon occur. Those changes come about through the power of love; they will be reflected in the linguistic transformations of the two sisters, principally those of Finea. Robert ter Horst argues that, while the "central event [of the play] unmistakably is Finea's awakening to the mind of love," *La dama boba* offers, like Finea, multiple layers of disguises ("The True Mind of Marriage" 347, 349). Our understanding of these levels necessarily involves Laurencio's role as both suitor and teacher to Finea. He transforms the "linda bestia" [beautiful dunce] into a shrewd woman by teaching her the power of love: "que es luz del entendimiento / amor" [love is the light of understanding] (1.10.830–31). The changes that Finea exhibits by the end of the play will be reflected in her linguistic virtuosity: she ultimately uses language as a device to accomplish her marriage to the man she loves.

Finea's transformation is a slow process. She occasionally regresses; for example, she ingenuously tells her father that Laurencio has written her love letters and even embraced her. Otavio warns his daughter not to allow herself to be embraced again: "Sólo vuestro marido ha de ser digno / de esos brazos" [Only your husband should be worthy / of your arms] (2.7.1527–28). His warning offers ironic possibilities for the future because Finea, as "boba," always functions on the literal level of linguistic meaning. In fact, in a subsequent scene, Finea offers Laurencio a solution to her father's concern: she allows him to "disembrace" her by repeating the action in reverse. In this example, Finea deduces that since "abrazar" [to embrace] is negative, "desabrazar" [disembrace] must be positive; she reveals her reasoning first in terms of verbal invention and then translates it into action. Consequently, Finea's solution leads not to an undoing, but to a redoing of the action that had gotten her into trouble with her father.

This scene offers the reader/spectator at least two possible readings. The first posits that Finea really *is* a beginning student at learning how language and linguistic control function: she cannot become an expert overnight. The dramatic action requires her to come to terms with language gradually by means of trial and error; her occasional steps backward would illustrate the evolutionary nature of her transformation. A second reading, however, would suggest a more ironic view of the scene. Finea's "disembracing" technique suggests that she may have assimilated Laurencio's lessons from this relatively early point in the play. Consequently, she quickly establishes herself as a controlling character by using her earlier linguistic ingenuousness as a means of effecting a repetition of the embrace.

Although apparently mutally exclusive, both readings are valid from a linguistic point of view. The "desabrazar" [disembrace] scene is significant because it explores how language works to transform and to control. It deals with the notion that the imaginative use of language, the invention of a verb like "desabrazar," can both resolve problems and create new ones—linguistic and otherwise—for the participants in a dialogue exchange. Moreover, even when speakers attempt to clarify the words they use, the end results are not always felicitous for the listeners in a conversation. Duardo and Nise proved this earlier in the sonnet scene. Finea proves it—to her father's dismay—here. As noted earlier, Melveena McKendrick has observed that Lope was well aware of the fact that "language has an infinite capacity to misinform, conceal, invent, leave ambiguous, and mislead" ("Language and Silence" 83). Finea's linguistic manipulation in *La dama boba* would certainly support those comments, while it also self-consciously reinforces the humor, irony, and multiple layers of meaning in the comedy.

No matter which interpretation of the scene described above is chosen, the *dama boba* is gradually changing as the result of Laurencio's lessons. Correspondingly, Nise begins to lose some of her earlier arrogance and confidence. When Nise notes the changes in her sister—"Yo te vi menos discreta" [You used to be less wise]—Finea responds, "Y yo más segura a ti" [And you were a lot more confident] (2.12.1672–73). Finea's new characterization reflects an increasing awareness of—and an appropriate correspondence between—language and action. As she sees her father approach, she decides—for the first time—to hold her tongue:

> Mi padre es éste; silencio.
> Callad lengua; ojos, hablad.

[Here comes my father: silence. / Tongue, hold on; eyes, your turn to speak.]

(2.15.1786–87)

As this example suggests, Finea now understands that remaining silent can also be a powerful tool for maintaining control in her life. The *dama boba* has thus learned the strategic value of speech and silence, both of which will serve her well in her quest to marry the man she loves.

Finea, however, still cannot match Laurencio's manipulations and linguistic skill. When she suggests falling out of love with him in order to end her jealousies, Laurencio offers a solution involving three important witnesses:

> Si dices delante destos
> cómo me das la palabra

de ser mi esposa y mujer,
todos los celos se acaban.

[If you speak in front of these people, / and give me your word / to be my wife / all jealousies will disappear.]

(2.18.1889–92)

Laurencio calls in his friends and servants to participate in his new deception, and Finea promises to marry him. The key point here involves the power of language—in all of its multiple levels—to manipulate. Laurencio not only deceives Finea with words, but he induces her to give him a verbal promise to marry:

Yo doy palabra
de ser esposa y mujer
de Laurencio.

[I give my word / to become the wife / of Laurencio.]

(2.18.1895–98)

It is important to note that Laurencio does not follow the *comedia* convention of asking Finea to give him her hand; rather, he stresses the power of language, used here in a witnessed agreement, to accomplish his goals.

Finea's promise to marry Laurencio relates to one of the central points of Austin's *How to Do Things with Words:* the division of utterances into performatives and constatives. The promise is clearly a performative, which "indicates that the issuing of the utterance is the performing of an action—it is not normally thought of as just saying something" (Austin 6–7). As we discussed above, in the latter part of *How to Do Things,* Austin replaces the performative-constative paradigm with the notion that discourse involves the negotiated, contextualized performance of certain kinds of acts (locutionary, illocutionary, and perlocutionary). The promise is later explained as a commissive utterance having illocutionary force, an utterance whose point "is to commit the speaker to a certain course of action" (157). Laurencio's manipulation of Finea via the promise is of primary importance in a Golden Age drama, since language was charged with such power by society and by its honor code in the literature of the epoch.

This lesson in linguistic manipulation is a major aspect of Finea's education. In the intervening month between acts 2 and 3, she obviously assimilates much more. As act 3 opens, Finea extols the virtues of her newfound love, for love has transformed her from *boba* [a simpleton] to *discreta* [a wise woman]. Yet, the theme of her soliloquy is not the only element that indicates a change in Finea. Her new sensibility surfaces as well in the type of language she employs, seen in her sophisticated use of metaphor, personification, and stylized baroque oppositions. In this soliloquy, Finea addresses love in a style designed to display her awareness of her new state of being:

Tú desataste y rompiste
la escuridad de mi ingenio;
tú fuiste el divino genio
que me enseñaste, y me diste
la luz con que me pusiste
el nuevo ser en que estoy.

[You untied and broke / the darkness of my wit / you were the divine force / who taught me, and gave me / the light with which you clothed me/ in this new state of being.]

(3.1.2053–58)

Finea has become so conscious of the power of language that she begins to show herself superior even to her teacher. She proposes a plan designed to rid herself of another suitor, Liseo; in the process, *she* becomes the controlling character and teacher:

El remedio es fácil.
Si, porque mi rudo ingenio,
que todos aborrecían,
se ha transformado en discreto,
Liseo me quiere bien,
con volver a ser tan necio
como primero le tuve,
me aborrecerá Liseo.

[The remedy is easy. / If Liseo now loves me / because my rude stupidity / that everyone loathed / is now transformed into wisdom / then, if I act as dumb / as I was at first / Liseo will loathe me again.]

(3.9.2478–86)

Finea succeeds admirably in feigning her previous state and deceiving Liseo. She cleverly returns to her former half-witted speech patterns, asking him such bizarre questions that the would-be suitor assumes she is crazy. He vows to return to Nise, concluding that Finea:

es loca sobre necia,
que es la peor guarnición.

[she's crazy on top of dumb / the worst garnish for a bad stew.]
(3.10.2610–11)

Finea's deception has been painful for her. After Liseo leaves and Laurencio returns, she exclaims:

siento en extremo
volverme a boba, aun fingida.
Y, pues fingida lo siento,
los que son bobos de veras,
¿cómo viven?
. . .
Háblame, Laurencio mío,
sutilmente, porque quiero
desquitarme de ser boba.

[I truly regret / being a simpleton again, even a fake one / And since I feel bad as a fake one / those who are real simpletons / how do they manage to live? / . . . / My dear Laurencio, speak to me / intelligently, because I want / to stop acting like such a simpleton.]
(3.11.2616–20; 2627–29)

Finea once more stresses language as the keystone of her new existence. She dupes Liseo by pretending to be her old (linguistic) self, but that experience threatens her new self, her new existence. Finea therefore begs Laurencio to reassure her that her newly acquired abilities, knowledge, and worth are truly hers. As a result, she returns to her new reality by appealing to Laurencio's ability to awaken her through language.

Finea's consciousness of her new state and her corresponding ability to control language are paralleled by Nise's awareness that she is losing control. In a telling scene with her father, she seeks to reestablish her position of superiority. Nise begins, "Yo quiero hablar claro," [I want to speak clearly] self-consciously calling attention to language's power, a power that Finea had also appealed to earlier. Her words are ironic, because although Nise pointedly promises to speak clearly, she uses this opportunity to manipulate her father by means of half-truths. She suggests that Otavio prevent Laurencio from entering their house, because her sister's suitor has obstructed Finea's marriage to Liseo and created strife in the family. Yet, the discreet Nise only reveals part of the truth. What she does not say is that she, herself, is jealous of the love that Laurencio and Finea share.

Recognizing that she is no longer in charge, Nise has thus attempted to reestablish her position of authority and superiority by using words to conceal and misinform. Her desperate attempts to restructure her world through the use of deceptive language, however, only further reveal her lack of control. She tries to play a linguistic game at which she is inexperienced; she is further sabotaged by the emotions that are overpowering her intellectual control.

The parallel between the two sisters here is striking. Both use words to manipulate, both show the precarious nature of their position, and both act out of love and/or jealousy. Yet Finea is helped by a loving confidant and teacher, while Nise is forced to act on her own. The links between language, emotion, and education are particularly marked in *La dama boba:* Finea begins the play using words without education, but with emotion; Nise's *métier* is the use of words without emotion, but *with* education. Both must approach a balance to end up as true *mujeres discretas* [wise women]. At this point, words, emotion, education, and control are beginning to merge for Finea; in Nise's case, though, gaps in her ability to combine these elements successfully will ultimately lead to failure.

Nise's efforts to change the course of the dramatic action are temporarily successful, for Otavio does attempt to remove Laurencio from his home. Laurencio, however, counters this strategy by announcing that he has been married to Finea for a month, because she had previously given him her word, her promise of marriage. Otavio claims that Finea was too dull to make such a promise—and to participate in such a social contract—and asks her a revealing question:

Otavio. Di, Finea:
¿no eres simple?
Finea. Cuando quiero.
Otavio. ¿Y cuando no?
Finea. No.

[*Otavio.* Tell me, Finea: / aren't you a simpleton? / *Finea.* Only when I want to be. / *Otavio.* And when you don't? *Finea.* Then I am not.]
(3.15.2795–97)

Finea's words should prepare Otavio for her final deception, but he refuses to heed the implications of her message.

Finea resolves to hide Laurencio by sending him to the attic and telling her father that he has gone to Toledo. Otavio exclaims that Finea is too naive to be trusted around men; he advises her to stay away from them forever. This advice fits Finea's plan perfectly, and she carefully leads her father into her trap by means of the conscious manipulation of words. Finea uses language to convey conflicting levels of meaning (literal and metaphoric) as she and her father discuss where she should hide from men. Finea suggests:

> ¿Será bien en un desván,
> donde los gatos están?
> ¿Quieres tú que allí me meta?

> [Do you think an attic will be good, / where I could keep company with the cats? / Do you want me to go there?]
>
> (3.18.2860–62)

Otavio replies that any place she chooses is acceptable, as long as no one else sees her. Finea is thus able to conclude triumphantly:

> Pues, ¡alto! En el desván sea;
> tú lo mandas, será justo.
> Y advierte que lo has mandado.

> [Well, then! To the attic; / you order it, so it must be right. / Remember that it was your idea]
>
> (3.18.2865–67)

Finea hurries off to obey her father's "order":

> No yerra quien obedece.
> No me ha de ver hombre más,
> sino quien mi esposo fuere.

> [In obedience lies no error. / No man shall ever see me again / except the one who will be my husband]
>
> (3.19.2876–78)

Finea has manipulated language to control the outcome of the dramatic action, proclaiming her innocence and obedience while she simultaneously arranges the details of her destiny.

As the play draws to a close, a servant rushes in with the news that two men are in the attic with Finea and her maid. Otavio runs off to defend his honor and threatens to kill Laurencio. Finea again assumes the controlling role as she explains her earlier "lie" that Laurencio was in Toledo:

Padre,
si aqueste desván se nombra
"Toledo," verdad le dije.
Alto está, pero no importa;
que más lo estaba el Alcázar
y la puente de Segovia
y hubo Juanelos que a él
subieron agua sin sogas.
¿El no me mandó esconder?
Pues suya es la culpa toda.

[Father, / if we name this attic / "Toledo," then I told the truth. / It is high, but that doesn't matter / for higher was the Alcazar / and the bridge of Segovia / and still there were people like the Juanelos / who managed to bring water up in buckets without rope. / Didn't he tell me to hide? / He's the only one to blame.]

(3.26.3129–38)

Finea succeeds in controlling language and in implementing her desires: the play ends with the promise of multiple weddings. Hence, it is fitting that words are the central elements of her plan, for Finea has learned about the power of language as a coproduct of the lessons of love she learned from Laurencio. As a result, she explains her enlightenment: "Por hablarte supe hablar . . . amor me ha enseñado" [Speaking to you I learned to speak . . . love taught me how"] (3.9.2467, 2473).[13] By means of the ultimate linguistic deception of naming her garret "Toledo," Finea has illuminated the arbitrary nature of the link between signifier and signified. Furthermore, she has illustrated how words can be used both in accordance with and against the linguistic conventions that govern discourse. Finea's manipulative use of words self-consciously underscores the power of language, calling attention to its fundamental importance in the comedy and showing us how language illuminates the oscillating movement between illusion and reality that has been a constant motif throughout the play.

Lope constantly calls our attention to the power of words. He pairs Nise's literary academies and analyses of esthetic language with Finea's ongoing lessons in how language functions and transforms as she changes. We have seen both principal and secondary characters use language self-consciously; Lope develops a subtle substructure based on language, on naming, on manipulation. When the women's suitors duel, they do so with words and not with swords. Direct references to language surface continually throughout the play. As certain characters seek to influence the actions of others, they express their desire in terms of language; "¡Nunca, plega a Dios, hablaras!" [May you never speak again, so help me God] or "¡Cortaréle aquella lengua!" [I'll cut that tongue off] are typical expletives. The characters of *La dama boba* play with the nature of discourse from the first scene to the last.

Nise's pedantic struggles with language and Finea's early ingenuous speech patterns and later intentional cleverness are devices used to create a comic effect. This creative use of words is, in many ways, similar to the type of witty exchanges found in other Golden Age comedies. What makes *La dama boba* particularly distinctive is an overwhelming emphasis on the communicative act itself. *La dama boba* is about control and manipulation, but it is primarily about how language effects that control. Lope implicitly encourages us to participate in the process of discovering how words function in the play, leading us to a kind of linguistic awareness that, not surprisingly, parallels the awakening of Finea to the potential of language.

2

Grice's Maxims and Rojas Zorrilla's *Entre bobos anda el juego*

> Speech-act theory is an account of the conditions of intelligibility, of what it means to mean in a community.
>
> —Stanley Fish

In the preceding analysis, we saw how language participates in constituting reality, how we can create worlds with words. On a most basic level, Rojas Zorrilla's comedy, *Entre bobos anda el juego* [*All the Players Were Fools*], is also a play about language. Yet, discourse in Rojas's comedy also functions differently: it calls attention to the idea that speakers are part of a community that shares certain ideas about how to perform. Sandy Petrey reminds us: "Words do things because a collectivity agrees on what they will do and the conditions under which they will do it" ("Speech Acts in Society" 44). The notion that a society establishes certain conventions for communication derives in part from the work of the linguist, H. Paul Grice. Grice's discussion of the conditions governing communication is the point of departure for this study of *Entre bobos anda el juego,* which moves beyond the idea that language can be the theme of the play toward an approach that emphasizes the relationship between language, society, and convention.

Following the lead of J. L. Austin, Grice explores the implications of the communicative act in his seminal article, "Logic and Conversation," the source of the basic terminology used in this analysis. His arguments begin with a definition of the Cooperative Principle, a rule governing all communicative behavior:

> Make your conversational contribution such as is required, at the stage at which it occurs, by the accepted purpose or direction of the talk exchange in which you are engaged. (45)

Effective communication results when all the participants in a speech exchange adhere to this guiding principle. This implies that those participants know about and (at least on a subconscious level) agree to these rules or maxims before speaking because they have grown up in a particular linguistic community. Petrey observes that speakers "accept prevailing community standards for verbal behavior" in a "collective acceptance of conventional procedures" ("Speech Acts in Society" 46, 51). Barbara Herrnstein Smith notes that we learn communicative rules by generalizing from previous experiences, adding that such conventions must be shared to be effective (*On the Margins* 99–100).

The maxims that Grice describes are a summary of the system of rules that guide the act of speaking. These rules direct the speaker who wants to communicate to be relevant and to the point, to tell the truth, and to give only the amount of information required to facilitate understanding. Specifically, Grice's model posits four categories of maxims inherent in each speech situation, which are summarized below:

> **Quantity** ("Make your contribution as informative as is required. Do not make your contribution more informative than is required."); **Quality** ("Try to make your contribution one that is true: Do not say what you believe to be false. Do not say that for which you lack adequate evidence."); **Relation** ("Be relevant."); **Manner** ("Be perspicuous: Avoid obscurity of expression. Avoid ambiguity. Be brief. Be orderly."). ("Logic and Conversation" 45–46)

Grice subsequently explores the types of possible violations of those maxims. Infrequently, a speaker may *unintentionally* fail to fulfill the maxims necessary for the successful functioning of the Cooperative Principle. More importantly, however, Grice discusses four cases in which a speaker *knowingly* fails to fulfill a maxim: when the speaker quietly and unostentatiously VIOLATES the maxim; when he refuses to participate and OPTS OUT of the speech act; when he is forced to violate at least one of the maxims because he is faced with a CLASH between two or more of them; when he blatantly FLOUTS the maxims (49).[1] Mary Louise Pratt reminds us that flouting is

> one of our favorite kinds of verbal play and . . . it is the only kind of intentional nonfulfillment possible in the literary speech situation. In literary works, intentionally failing to observe a maxim always counts as flouting. (*Toward a Speech Act Theory* 160)

Grice's ideas on the nature of communication have a great deal to do with what happens in literature and specifically with what happens in drama. In literary texts in general (just as in nonliterary discourse), characters give information by flouting these maxims; they characterize or define themselves (at least in part) via their linguistic behavior by following or defying the rules of their community of speakers. The situation is even more complex in the theater. The "new" message resulting from the nonobservance of the maxims governing conversation operates on two levels: with regard to the discourse exchanged between characters onstage and with regard to the audience in the theater. This double layering of discourse serves to remind the audience of its own esthetic position within the theatrical experience.[2] This suggests that linguistic violations occurring onstage may prove to be felicitous in the extreme for members of the audience.

Grice's thesis—that breaking the rules governing discourse in a community can be just as significant (and as commonplace) as following them—would indicate that the study of drama can also utilize this model for a more explicit reason: the ideal state, the philosophy that guides the Cooperative Principle, simply does not function for every character and every situation in a medium that thrives on conflict. Dramatic action is based on conflict; the *comedia*—and, particularly, *comedias de capa y espada* [cloak and sword plays], *comedias de enredo* [plays with complicated intrigue], and the case here, *comedias de figurón* [*comedias* with a pretentious and extravangant fool at the center]—is founded upon misunderstandings, conscious deceit, and confusion. If all the characters in these plays fully observed the Cooperative Principle, it would be much more difficult—if not impossible—to define and establish the dramas' conflicts.

The central concerns of comedy are often the points at which communication breaks down and conflicts are defined, points that could be described as moments when Grice's maxims are not observed. We should not, however, prejudge such rule breaking. Pratt emphasizes this issue: "the maxims are anything but ironclad. In fact, they are honored as often in the breach as in the observance" (*Toward a Speech Act Theory* 132). What this suggests is that rule breaking in and of itself should not be labeled as positive or negative; it should be described, rather than prescribed or proscribed.[3] Consequently, the study of rule deviation is particularly useful for interpretation because of the special nature of discourse in the theater, and especially in comedy. William Dodd explains that

> the use of the tools of conversational analysis may help to throw light on the way the dramatic action is vehicled in the "here and now" of the verbal interaction structure. . . . What the studies of discourse analysts, conversationalists and language philosophers can offer us here is a set of instruments with which to identify and "measure" these deviances more accurately. ("Conversation" 181, 185)

Grice's description of rule breaking within linguistic communities therefore provides us with a model for identifying and measuring these deviances. By examining the Cooperative Principle both in the observance and in the breach, we can encounter new ways to analyze dramatic texts from a fresh perspective. An analysis of the communicative attempts that succeed—as well as those that fail—can help to explain conflicts and delineate the relationship between language, theme, and characterization.

Grice's ideas on linguistic competence and communities of speakers can help to explicate Golden Age dramas in a number of ways. By cataloging the types of exchanges that establish characterization, we can see patterns that emerge between and among the characters based on their linguistic behavior. These patterns of verbal behavior relate to rule breaking (and its effects on other interlocutors), silence, turn-taking, etc. Such discussions can help to define the cosmovision of a particular dramatist within his or her community and epoch, complementing more traditional readings of a dramatist's literary corpus. In general, Golden Age dramatists lay bare the very concepts that Grice has articulated by underscoring the flouting of linguistic deviance or rule breaking. Consequently, an understanding of the relationship between linguistic conventions and behavior helps to clarify basic aspects of the dramatic text. We can use this type of approach to study not simply how characters break the rules of communication, but what happens as a result, what Sandy Petrey calls the performative nature of speech versus consequences ("Speech Acts in Society" 48), which will always be seen from the perspective of viewing an utterance in context.

* * *

Grice's maxims and his notion of the Cooperative Principle are central to this analysis of Francisco de Rojas Zorrilla's *Entre bobos anda el juego* (c. 1638) and, as such, can help us "move from intuition to a linguistically-justified response to a drama text" (Burton, *Dialogue* 5). In *Entre bobos,* the Cooperative Principle's "firing" and "misfiring" could be seen as a virtual precondition to the play's existence. In a very real sense, Rojas's play parallels Shakespeare's *Corolianus,* which Stanley Fish describes as being

> about speech acts, the rules of their performance, the price one pays for obeying those rules, the impossibility of ignoring or refusing them and still remaining a member of the community. It is also about what the theory is about, language and its power. . . . ("How to Do Things" 244)

By exploring the speech acts that succeed and fail in *Entre bobos,* by analyzing how communicative rules are obeyed or ignored, we may gain added insight into the relationships existing among the various characters and may then be better able to integrate the comedy's complex plot with its characterizations.[4]

In *Entre bobos anda el juego,* linguistic deviance and rule breaking function as the axis upon which the comedy turns. The basic situation involves a young woman, Doña Isabel, whose father has arranged her marriage to an obnoxious, but rich, older man (Don Lucas). Isabel manages to get together with her true love, the impoverished Pedro, by the end of act 3, but the lovers suffer their own share of mishaps along the road to marriage, most of which result from the ways they use words.

Each character's linguistic behavior reveals a specialized ability or lack thereof. Isabel and Pedro are adept at formal debate; Don Luis, the ridiculous suitor whose love is completely unrequited, produces verbose *cultismos* [learned expressions]; and Don Lucas, the play's principal *figurón* [pretentious fool],[5] embodies a similarly affected verbosity, as well as vulgar materialism, in much of his discourse. Given the conventions of comedy and our intuitions regarding linguistic ability and superiority, we might expect that the young, linguistically adept lovers would be united in marriage and live happily ever after. This is only partially true. Actually, the final scene of the play turns the expectations of the characters—and of the audience—upside down. We have been led to believe that the play proceeds along the lines of classic comedy, in which the obstacle, the blocking character, will be chastized or made the fool, thus removing him as an impediment to the lovers. Suddenly, however, Don Lucas tricks the tricksters. How and why this happens, how language works onstage as well as between the world of the stage and that of the audience, will be the focus of this analysis.

The preceding discussion suggests that language becomes a

central aspect of both the characters' definitions and their destinies, although, since Rojas has written a comedy, he presents such serious ideas within the framework of the ridiculous. Raymond MacCurdy lends support to the significance of this interplay between comedy and language in *Entre bobos:*

> *Entre bobos anda el juego* shows to good advantage the persistent traits of Rojas' great gift for comic talent: a keen sense of the ludicrous, a gift for caricature, and resourcefulness in manipulating language for humorous effect. (*Spanish Drama* 517)

What becomes apparent is that the unique linguistic styles of each of the characters in the play underline "Rojas' great gift for comic talent," joining to illuminate the interplay of dramatic speech and dramatic action and illustrating how language can serve as a powerful weapon in the battle of the sexes.

The links between characterization, plot, and theme in *Entre bobos* are clearly related to the ways that communication is effected or subverted onstage in Rojas's comedy. Linguistic manipulation lies at the heart of many of the communicative acts of the play. It manifests itself in two distinct ways: as the key element in the debates between the heroine, Doña Isabel, and the *galán,* Don Pedro, and as the explicit means of characterizing the play's two *figurones,* Don Lucas and Don Luis. Each of the four characters mentioned above relishes the manipulation of language, seen in speech acts whose purpose is to illuminate the speaker's linguistic virtuosity; and each will play an important role in the crucial final scene. Before we can properly understand that last example of linguistic manipulation, however, we need to analyze how Rojas leads his audience up to that point.

As the play opens, Isabel and her servant take opposing sides in a debate dealing with the advantages and disadvantages of marriage; the servant prefers lovers, while Isabel insists that husbands are better, even though they may not shower their wives with deceitful flattery:

> menos habla quien más siente,
> más quiere quien calla más.
> No esa llama solicito,
> todo lenguas al arder,
> porque un amor bachiller
> tiene indicios de apetito;

[he who feels more speaks less, / he who is most silent loves more. / I don't want this flame, / all tongues afire, / because a love that is all words / contains more than a hint of lust.]

(1.63–68)

Doña Isabel's speech is exemplary in this first scene because it sets the tone for the rest of the play. She loves to debate, urging her servant to change her mind, based on the "sound" arguments that she offers:

Lo contrario he de creer
de lo que arguyendo estás,
y de mi atención verás . . .
. . .
Y ansí mi opinión verás
de mi argumento evidente. . . .

[I have to believe / the opposite of what you're arguing / and from my remarks you will notice . . . / . . . / And so, you'll see how right I am / because my argument is so evident. . . .]

(1.49–51, 61–62)

The emphasis on the language of argument and debate is thus established from this first scene. Isabel firmly fixes the tone of the comedy by underscoring the importance of language in her own characterization, by stressing the use of verbal thrusting and parrying, and by insisting that she in linguistically superior.

Doña Isabel's love of debate will reappear as a unifying motif in later scenes with Don Pedro. Rojas contrasts this presentation of linguistic virtuosity with the verbal and written misfirings of the two *figurones,* Don Lucas and Don Luis. These two men, both unwelcome suitors of Doña Isabel, illustrate how language may be used to create humor and to characterize with precision. Their violations of the Cooperative Principle in almost every utterance are clearly humorous. We note the ironic disparity between the intended effects of the language they use and those actually achieved; we laugh because we are distanced from (and superior to) the disintegrating communication we witness.

Don Luis, one of the caricatures presented by Rojas in *Entre bobos,* will be described in detail later in this analysis. The principal *figurón* is Doña Isabel's fiancé, Don Lucas. Don Lucas's servant paints a portrait of his master, describing him as

zambo un poco, calvo un poco,
dos pocos verdimoreno,

tres pocos desaliñado
y cuarenta muchos puerco.

[a bit bow-legged, and a bit bald, / two bits swarthy, / three bits unkempt / and forty times dirtier than swine]

(1.217–20)

Don Lucas is, in summary,

mal poeta, peor ingenio,
mal músico, mentiroso,
preguntador sobre necio.

[a bad poet, his wit is even duller, / bad as a musician, a liar, / and on top of being stupid, he's always asking too many questions.]

(1.254–56)

Moreover, he is so stingy that, according to his servant, "no tiene excrementos" [he doesn't even produce excrement] (1.266). Don Lucas revels in "topping" every story he hears; he may be stingy with money, but he is a spendthrift with words:

a cada palabra que habla
aplica dos o tres cuentos,
verdad es que son muy largos,
mas para eso no son buenos;
no hay lugar donde no diga
que ha estado, ninguno ha hecho
cosa que le cuente a él
que él no la hiciese primero.

[for every word he speaks / he uses two or three examples— / it's true that they are very long, / but that doesn't mean they're good; / there is no place he says / he hasn't been, and nobody has done / anything that he didn't do first.]

(1.233–40)

As the servant's comments emphasize, the effect of this overblown language on Lucas's listeners within the play is disastrous. The fact that Don Lucas constantly flouts the maxims of Quantity (giving more information than is required) and Manner (being unnecessarily prolix) contributes greatly to his listeners' negative reactions.

Doña Isabel does not even need to experience her fiancé's linguistic misfirings to be set against marrying him. She has already fallen in love with Don Lucas's cousin, Don Pedro, who is the antithesis of his rich relative. Indeed, although penniless, Don Pedro is a paradigm of virtue. Whereas Don Lucas writes bad plays, Don Pedro is a "Lope," arguably the greatest dramatist of the Golden Age. Pedro counters Lucas's stinginess by being so generous that he gives and does not tell that he has given. Lucas, then, is the miser who uses *language* to build his ego and reputation; Pedro is the admirable character whose *deeds* speak for him.

Don Lucas underscores the role of language in *Entre bobos anda el juego* in his letters to Isabel and her father. These self-conscious texts—written discourse within the larger frame of dramatic oral discourse—call attention to themselves by the degree to which they differ from the rest of the verbal texts in the play. In this sense, the use of epistolary prose within the text of the comedy automatically forces us to focus on those letters, giving them a greater degree of importance than more "ordinary" speech acts receive.[6] In addition, the letters foreground their own physical presence in the play because they require one character to pause and read them aloud, while other characters do nothing but stop and listen. The letters thus create rich representational possibilities. Conversation—dialogue—ceases, and the characters who are listening concentrate on their own physical reaction(s) and response(s) to the letters. The letters therefore help to emphasize a variety of levels of interpretation, just as their content works to illuminate the character of Don Lucas.

Don Lucas's letters of introduction are literally vehicles for his own self-characterization. Apart from introducing himself to Isabel, Don Lucas apparently intends to impress her with the subject of greatest interest to him—money. He begins his first letter by explaining that he has 6,042 *ducados* [ducats] that will go to his cousin if he (Lucas) fails to have any children. Lucas then proposes that Isabel meet him at a nearby inn in order to begin making future heirs to inherit all of this money. Don Lucas thus reveals himself as "practical" in the extreme—he does not want to wait one minute to start creating the children who will inherit his money.

By expressing himself in this manner, however, Don Lucas ignores social conventions and the honor code in order to use Doña Isabel's "services." He leaves his listeners with the impression that Isabel will be regarded only as valuable land that, properly used (that is, fertilized), will produce equally valuable crops. His proposition devalues Isabel's reputation within the Spanish society of the time; this moral devaluation ironically contrasts with

Don Lucas's inflated self-portrait, which was intended to impress Isabel with his wealth.

Don Lucas's language and manner of expression in this letter and the one that follows convey a different message to his audience than that originally intended. After hearing Lucas's first letter read aloud, his listeners conclude that Don Lucas is a coarse beast; his second letter confirms their appraisal. This letter to Isabel's father is, in essence, a receipt for his daughter:

> Recebí de don Antonio de Salazar una mujer, para que lo sea mía, con sus tachas buenas o malas, alta de cuerpo, pelimorena y doncella de facciones, y la entregaré tal y tan entera, siempere que me fuere pedida por nulidad o divorcio. En Toledo, a 4 de setiembre de 638 años.—*Don Lucas del Cigarral.* Toledo.

[From Don Antonio de Salazar I have received a woman, with the intention to make her my wife, with all her features, be they good or bad, tall in body, dark haired and young looking; I will surrender her just as she is now if I am required to do so due to annulment or divorce. Sworn in Toledo, 4 September, 1638. *Don Lucas del Cigarral.* Toledo.]

Like the first letter, this minitext causes the listeners onstage to exclaim over Don Lucas's boorish behavior. Don Lucas has violated the rules governing communicative behavior and social convention; his linguistic behavior, like his exaggerated physical behavior, is typical of the traditional Spanish Golden Age *figurón.*

Inherent in the ideas of linguistic communities and verbal conventions is the notion of the social contract. As B. H. Smith reminds us, "every linguistic transaction is also a social transaction" (*On the Margins* 101). In *Entre bobos,* Rojas has taken this idea an ironic step further. Don Lucas continually breaks the rules that constitute his contacts with the linguistic community. What is ironic is that the receipt that he sends to Don Antonio, in itself a type of contract, shows that Don Lucas is out of step with his community of speakers; his social contracts, whether expressed orally or in writing, subvert his intentions, making him appear ill-mannered rather than desirable.

Don Lucas's linguistic style may be compared to that of Don Luis, Isabel's long-suffered and long-suffering suitor. If Don Lucas's linguistic behavior is devaluating and materialistic, Don Luis's speech is either pompous, ridiculous, or off the subject as in the following exchange between Luis and his servant, Carranza:

Carranza. Di, ¿qué tienes, señor?
Luis. Desvalimiento.
Carranza. Deja de hablar afeitado,
y dime: ¿a qué propósito has llegado
a estas ventas?

. . .

Luis. Pues a mi voz te pido
que hagas un agasajo con tu oído:
Carranza amigo, yo me hallé inclinado,
costóme una deidad casi un cuidado;
mentalmente la dije mi deseo;
aspiraba a los lazos de Himeneo,
y ella, viendo mi amor enternecido,
se dejó tratar mal del dios Cupido.

[*Carranza.* What's wrong, sir? Tell me.
Luis. I am woefully helpless.
Carranza. Stop your fancy talk
and tell me: what's your purpose
in coming to this inn?

. . .

Luis. I only ask,
that you offer my voice the gift of your ears:
my friend Carranza, I felt an inclination,
a deity made me spend all my cares
I told her, mentally, my wish;
I aspired to the Himenaean bonds
but she, seeing my tender love for her
allowed herself to be abused by the god Cupid.]

(1.552–55, 561–70)

Luis's love complaint is so ridiculous, so linguistically muddled, that Carranza responds:

Oí tu relación, y maravilla
que con cuatro vocablos de cartilla,
todos impertinentes,
me digas tantas cosas diferentes.

[I heard your story, and I marvel / that with a few words from a reader's primer / all of them impertinent / you still manage to tell me so many different things.]

(1.607–10)

In Isabel's characterization of Don Luis, she also details her affected suitor's abuses of language. As the following example suggests, Don Luis becomes even more unbearable to her each time he opens his mouth:

> Nunca entabla
> lenguaje disparatado;
> antes, por hablar cortado,
> corta todo lo que habla;
> vocablos de estrado son
> con los que a obligarme empieza:
> dice "crédito," "fineza,"
> "recato," "halago," "atención"
> y desto hace mezcla tal,
> que aun con amor no pudiera
> digerirlo, aunque tuviera
> mejor calor natural.

> [He never speaks / with foolish language; / to keep from being tongue-tied, he ties up every word he utters; / he polishes everything he says; / he uses parlor words / to do me a favor: / he says "credit," "finery," "discretion," "pleasantry," "attention" / and he makes such a mess of all of this / that although I were in love with him, I wouldn't be able / to digest it, even if I had / a better natural disposition]
>
> (1.122–32)

Don Luis's cultured vocabulary and affected style are, certainly, perceived by Isabel as undesirable qualities. Viewed from the perspective of Grice's model, Luis—like Don Lucas—violates many of the maxims necessary for the Cooperative Principle to function effectively. These violations of the maxims governing communication parody the literary lover's attempts to win over his beloved.[7] Don Luis's speech exchanges are not felicitous, and the result is that he unconsciously transforms the communicative act from one of affection to one of disaffection.

Don Luis calls attention to language—and to himself in unwanted ways—with every polished and affected phrase. His self-conscious failures to impress with words create two distinct results for the reader/spectator. The first is to reinforce the powerful role of language as both a creative and destructive force in *Entre bobos*. The second result is to facilitate the expression of humor. Luis's inappropriate speech acts are not only funny in and of themselves, but they acquire increased comic potential as we view the other characters' reactions to what Don Luis says. In the following exchange, Luis's servant, Carranza, reacts to his master's artificial style of speaking with some scatological wordplay:

Luis. Gente cursa el camino. ¿Si ha llegado?
Carranza. ¿Qué es cursa? ¿Este camino está purgado?

[*Luis.* People are coursing through the path. Hath she arrived? / *Carranza.* What is coursing? Has this road been purged?]

(1.611–12)

Even Don Lucas cannot deal with the extremes of Don Luis's ridiculous use of speech, as in the following example, in which Lucas reacts to an absurd description of Isabel:

Luis. Digo que adoré sus rayos
con amor tan pertinaz. . . .
Lucas. ¿Pertinaz? Don Luis, ¿queréis
que me vaya agora a echar
en el pozo de Cabañas
que en esa plazuela está?

[Luis. I say that I adored the rays (of her hair) / with such a stubborn love . . . / *Lucas.* Stubborn? Don Luis, do you want me / to go now and throw / myself in the Cabañas well, / the one that's in that little square over there?]

(3.2519–24)

Don Luis is truly a comic character; his speech and actions create humor, and their comic effect is only multiplied by the appalled reactions of the other characters onstage. Most importantly, the basis for all of Luis's comic characterization is his mishandling of language and the communicative act: he is a character whose linguistic abuses form the essence of his characterization.

The ridiculous verbal posturing by Don Luis and Don Lucas contrasts with the linguistic play of the love scenes between Pedro and Isabel. As previously noted, Pedro and Isabel have met before and have fallen instantly in love. Further, because he is Lucas's cousin, Pedro has the opportunity to see Isabel often. Just as in *La dama boba* [*The Lady Simpleton*], the two lovers hide their love from the rest of the characters throughout most of the play, revealing their passion only in their private love scenes. Unlike *La dama boba,* however, these scenes frequently turn into love debates. These two characters are artists whose medium is language. Their verbal duelling—for example, over Pedro's praise of Isabel's beauty—demonstrates their conscious delight in manipulating language. Each character parries the verbal thrusts of the other so well that we conclude that the two are evenly matched, at least linguistically. This linguistic match between Pedro and Isabel contrasts with the inequality of the relationship between Isabel and Don Lucas, which is made manifest in Don Lucas's love letters, a parody of a lover's first communication with his intended bride. The humor is heightened when Don Lucas asks his cousin to speak to Isabel in his place, à la Cyrano de Bergerac. Pedro replaces Don Lucas verbally, just as he intends to do physically.

While in the guise of speaking for his cousin, Don Pedro declares his love for Isabel, and she offers him her hand. The reader/spectator can appreciate the subtleties of this scene; only the two young lovers know the literal implications of their linguistic play as they openly deceive Don Lucas. Yet, after a while, even Don Lucas finally begins to become suspicious:

Lucas. Primillo, fondo en cuñado,
idos un poco a la lengua.
Pedro. ¡Si yo hablaba aquí por vos!
Lucas. Sois un hablador, y ella
es también otra habladora.
Isabel. ¡Si vos me disteis licencia!
Lucas. Sí, pero sois licenciosa.

[*Lucas.* Dear cousin, a brother-in-law at heart, / spill the beans. / *Pedro.* But I was speaking here on your behalf! / *Lucas.* You are a talkative fellow, and she / is a talkative one, too. / *Isabel.* You gave me license to speak! / *Lucas.* Yes, but you are licentious.]

(1.893–99)

Once again, a dialogue exchange self-referentially uses language as both its subject and object. The characters' constant references to words both express a recognition of the fact that language can be world-creating and signal further conflict at the plot level.

In the final half of the play, comic manipulation of language combines with physical humor. Rojas employs the Golden Age convention of having his characters stumble into each other in the dark. Consequently, as the play progresses, mistaken identities and intentions combine with the linguistic and physical humor of *Entre bobos* to create a richly woven, textured comedy.

As the different pairs of characters trip over each other in the dark, their equally confused conversation further complicates the plot. Specifically, the two lovers, Pedro and Isabel, become jealous of each other. They continue their love debates, but the tone has changed, due to the overwhelming number of quarrels they have. Pedro and Isabel speak without thinking and react without adequate evidence to support their reactions. Their failures to observe the rules guiding communication are clearly intentional: these characters are interested not in the facts, but in the debate itself. The preconditions necessary for felicitous communication[8] to occur are absent; the lovers' apparent interest in continuing to debate stems from their ability to control language in stating their respective cases.

We may best observe the tenor of these debates in act 3. In the following scene, Pedro overreacts after misinterpreting an exchange between Isabel and Luis. He jealously views their relationship as a love affair; here, he responds to Isabel, firmly taking the offensive:

> Písdeme celos agora
> de doña Alfonsa, Isabel.
> Habla. ¿Qué te ha suspendido?
> No finjas leves enojos;
> di que no han visto mis ojos,
> de que está incapaz mi oído.
> Resuelto a escucharte estoy.
> ¿Qué puedes ya responder?

[Tell me now that you are jealous / of Doña Alfonsa, Isabel. / Talk. Why are you silent? / Don't pretend you are annoyed; / say that my eyes have not seen what they saw, / say that my ears are disabled. / I am resolved to listen to you. / What do you say now?]

(3.2283–90)

Pedro's speech is a classic example of the communicative act gone awry. It blends manipulation with overreliance on the all-too-fallible senses. Although Pedro says that he is resolved to listen to Isabel's explanation, his tone and his repeated commands force us to doubt that conclusion. He therefore blatantly sets up a linguistic situation that precludes real communication.

Isabel counters Pedro's accusations by refusing to argue. She proposes to give him satisfaction only:

Isabel. Con ser quien soy.

. . .

Isabel. Con callar.

. . .

Isabel. Con decir que te amo a ti.

. . .

Isabel. A callar me sentencio.

[*Isabel.* By being who I am. / . . . / *Isabel.* By keeping quiet. / . . . / *Isabel.* By saying that I love you. / . . . / *Isabel.* I sentence myself to be silent.] (3.2292, 2296, 2300, 2301)

This nonparticipation strategy is a key change of technique on Isabel's part. (Grice defines this technique as the deliberate opting out of the speech exchange). By refusing to speak, Isabel effectively tries to communicate to Pedro that he should trust her and that she owes him no further explanations. This strategy, however, has its consequences. Don Pedro rejects her silence and responds by leaving in anger:

¿No crees tú en mis palabras,
y he de creer tu silencio?
. . .
Ya no he de ser el que soy;
ya no quiere, arrepentido,
sufrir a tu voz mi oído:
ya te dejo, ya me voy.

[So you don't believe my words / and I have to believe your silence? / . . . / I will no longer be the one I am now; / my ear, regretfully, does not want / to suffer your voice any more: / I'm leaving you, I am gone.] (3.2303–5, 2321–24)

Once again, the two lovers can use neither speech nor silence to communicate effectively due, in no small part, to the fact that they really refuse to listen to each other. Rather, their debates are exhibitions of language designed to create specific effects. The lovers' speeches are all one-sided, since each character is more interested in making points and winning the debate than in communicating in a give-and-take relationship.

We know that Pedro and Isabel love each other; we suspect that they will eventually be united. Our interest in them, then, must derive from admiration—or, at least, understanding—of their linguistic ability and the delight that they show in exploring the potential of language. At the same time, however, the overwhelming frequency of their amorous debates subtly begins to prepare us for the comedy's ironic ending.

The effect of these debates on the audience influences our reading of the final scenes of the play. If we look upon these debating scenes as necessary to the resolution of the comedy, we will not be overly troubled by the outcome. However, it is also possible to tire of the two characters' pointless sparring. If this second reaction obtains, we may conclude that Pedro and Isabel are much less sympathetic characters than they were before their long series of debates. Their verbal duels show off their linguistic ability, but that ultimately barren ability loses its allure when the "lovers" repeatedly refuse to listen to each other, refuse to take turns speaking, and interrupt each other at will. Consequently, our interpretation of these debates necessarily influences our opinion of the felicity of the play's conclusion and our analysis of the function of poetic justice in the comedy.

Although the physical action and final speeches of the minor characters are exceedingly funny, the play does not end on a note of good-natured humor. The last scenes lead us to a rapid, though cynical, resolution of the complexities of the main plot involving Don Lucas, Don Pedro, and Doña Isabel. Don Lucas, the *figurón,* has finally realized that his cousin and his intended bride are in love, that they have been manipulating him, and that they have been playing him for a fool. He gathers all of the characters together for a final confrontation. At this point, the linguistic style of the play changes abruptly. Don Lucas issues a series of crisp orders to the assembled characters, calling them to attention. He is now in charge, controlling language and creating a staccato effect that forces his fellow characters to listen carefully:

Lucas. Cerrad la puerta.
Cabellera. Ya cierro.
Lucas. Dadme la llave.
Cabellera. Tomad.
Lucas. Don Luis, salid.
Luis. Ya yo salgo.

[*Lucas.* Close the door. / *Cabellera.* I'm closing it. / *Lucas.* Give me the key. / *Cabellera.* Here it is. / *Lucas.* Don Luis, leave. / *Luis.* I'm leaving.] (3.2635–37)

Don Lucas explains the situation as he perceives it and unravels all of the threads of the complicated plot. He lists the examples of Pedro and Isabel's "betrayal" one by one, until the young lovers break down and confess their love for each other; at this point, Pedro, now repentant, asks Don Lucas to put him to death: "Estrene el cuchillo ya / en mi garganta" [Try out your knife / on my throat] (3.2716–17). Don Lucas, however, has other plans:

Eso no;
yo no os tengo de matar;
eso es lo que vos queréis.

[Not that; / I'm not going to kill you; / that's just what you want]
(3.2717–19)

Through his manipulation of these characters, Don Lucas has led his onstage audience to the dramatic climax. He then coldly and methodically outlines the details of his plan for revenge. Lucas mandates that since both Pedro and Isabel are penniless, their punishment will be to marry. Their poverty will lead to unhappiness: although their passion will fade, their need will remain constant. Lucas again intentionally plays with language itself to explain how his curse will live with the couple forever:

de mí os vengáis esta noche,
y mañana, a más tardar,
cuando almuercen un requiebro,
y en la mesa, en vez de pan,
pongan una "fe" al comer
y una "constancia" al cenar,
y, en vez de galas, se ponga
un buen amor de Milán,
una tela de "mi vida,"
aforrada en "¿me querrás?"
echarán de ver los dos
cuál se ha vengado de cuál.

[You take revenge on me tonight, / and tomorrow, at the latest, / when they have an endearment for breakfast / and on the table, instead of bread, / they lay out "faith" for lunch / and "constancy" for dinner, / and, instead of fine clothes, she wears / good Milan love, / material made of "you are my life" / and lining made of "will you love me always?" / both of them will realize then / who has taken revenge on whom.]
(3.2741–53)

Lucas's cynical words suggest the ultimate use of language: it must serve as food and clothing for the penniless couple.

Lucas thus proves that he is not the fool that we had believed him to be. He manipulates speech self-consciously, much as Doña Finea did in *La dama boba,* in order to expose language as object.[9]

In doing so, Lucas demonstrates that the lovers who played with language so ably in the early parts of the play will now both literally and figuratively have to eat their own words. The controllers have become the "controlled," and the plot ends on an ironic note.

The inverted ending returns us to A. A. Parker's notion of poetic justice.[10] In a very literal sense, each character gets what he or she deserves. Pedro and Isabel are united in love, but they suffer financial doom because of the way they schemed and lied. Luis marries a minor comic figure, the sister of Don Lucas. Lucas knowingly forswears marriage and is left with the partner he chooses: revenge.

If we reconsider the debates between Isabel and Pedro, we are not surprised by the "punishment" that they receive at the hands of Don Lucas. The two lovers ably manipulate words, but from a very egocentric perspective. Their inability to be good listeners as they continually try to out-talk each other shows them to be fundamentally self-centered. Consequently, they merit Don Lucas's vengeance; their punishment conforms to A. A. Parker's definition of poetic justice. It is thus ironically fitting that the verbal masters must now literally eat their own words. The two lovers are joined in marriage, but it will be a marriage characterized by their own innate linguistic qualities.

The principal unifying element of this comedy is the manipulation of language within the linguistic community, which serves to complement the plot, characterization, and theme of *Entre bobos anda el juego*.[11] The speech act is constantly on display, and the play's unusual ending illustrates how linguistic control functions. In order to explain further this deviation from the conventionalized norms of society, we may return again to Grice.

It is clear that the Cooperative Principle as described by Grice does not work successfully in *Entre bobos*. His four maxims (*quality, quantity, relation,* and *manner*) are consistently violated by the characters of the play. Pedro and Isabel quietly violate the maxim of quality when they deceive Don Lucas. Their incessant love debates illustrate numerous clashes between the maxims: the debaters cannot be brief and orderly (the maxim of manner), because they try too hard to score linguistic points, thereby giving too much information to each other (the maxim of quantity), while, in addition, they do not stop to listen. The end of the play marks an obvious change in Isabel's linguistic comportment. When she finally refuses to debate any longer, she opts out of the dialogue and ceases to communicate (at least on a verbal level). Her decision to opt out raises new questions regarding the role of silence in such a discourse-oriented play and regarding the relationship between such a verbal strategy and the eternal battle between the sexes (including questions of female discourse). Isabel's two comic suitors, Don Lucas and Don Luis, flout all of the maxims in their exaggerated, overblown presumption. Consequently, these caricatures incarnate just what happens when words are uttered without a concomitant understanding of "what it means to mean in a community" (Fish, "How to Do Things" 245).

Our discussion of dramatic discourse explores and underscores the interrelationship of the communicative acts of *Entre bobos* and illustrates how Rojas has woven the threads of the early parts of the play into a coherent whole. The kinds of maxims violated and the nature and number of those violations give us more specific information and more specific tools for describing the linguistic behavior of Rojas's characters. In other words, Grice's model allows us to substantiate our arguments regarding linguistic manipulation with a more precise vocabulary. It further enables us to examine the results of that manipulation (i.e., the flouting of maxims), and can lead to a clearer understanding of Don Lucas's ironic punishment involving language at the end of the comedy. Finally, the model allows us to compare and contrast the linguistic transactions that occur within the community of speakers who populate this comedy and to relate the ways that those characters comport themselves with words to the larger issues of the production of meaning outside the world of the theater as well.

As we note the importance of language in the play, we observe its use in creating humor. At times we laugh because the characters who best control language allow us to join in the laughter at another character's expense. At other times, as Mary Louise Pratt notes, we "delight in the imaginative exercise of calculating 'what's really going on'" (*Toward a Speech Act Theory* 199). Ultimately, however, we are invited to discover how Rojas's ironic ending creates comedy. The resolution of the play blends marriage and its intrinsic promise of rebirth with an accurate portrait of human foibles. All of these multiple levels surface in the foregrounding of language and the communicative act. We have seen that this play, again borrowing a phrase from Stanley Fish, is "about what language is about" (221). *Entre bobos anda el juego* illuminates the intentional and unintentional thwarting of the communicative act, the ways our words affect other people, and the making of meaning. Rojas's excursion into the world of comedy treats a number of serious issues. As we have found, the contributions of linguistic philosophers such as Grice have allowed us to explore what it is that makes us laugh, as well as why we are still able to do so some three hundred and fifty years after the play was written.

3

Labels and Lies: Names and Don García's World in *La verdad sospechosa*

> One of the main purposes for which we use language is the purpose of stating facts about things and persons and events. If we want to fulfill this purpose, we must have some way of forestalling the question, "What (who, which one) are you talking about?" as well as the question, "What are you saying about it (him, her)?"
>
> —P. F. Strawson

Speech act theory covers a broad range of topics. Our analysis of *La dama boba* focused on the thematic possibilities of having language act to transform reality. With *Entre bobos anda el juego,* we examined the kinds of social contracts that come out of linguistic transactions, and we explored the relationship between rule breaking and the place that dramatic characters occupy in the fictive society of which they are a part. In that context, Grice's notion of the Cooperative Principle and his communicative maxims gave us the tools to examine Rojas Zorrilla's play from a fresh perspective. The following analysis, however, is less oriented toward a specific speech act theory of literary discourse: our study of Juan Ruiz de Alarcón's *La verdad sospechosa* is most closely allied with general philosophical debates on the nature of reference and on the theatrical implications of naming.

Ruiz de Alarcón's *La verdad sospechosa* [*The Suspect Truth*], about an inveterate liar who is forced to marry a woman he does not love, was long considered the model for teaching moral circumspection. The majority of critical studies of the play have dealt both with García's motivation for lying and with the interpretation of the play's ambiguous ending.[1] It is interesting to note, however, that a number of French critics have taken a different approach in discussing Pierre Corneille's *Le Menteur* [*The Liar*]; their perspective reveals a keen interest in the nature of dramatic discourse,[2] an area to which (at least to date) Hispanists have devoted less time. In our linguistically oriented reading of *La verdad sospechosa,* we will examine the question of reference, specifically, García's insistent naming of himself. In the play, García assumes multiple identities, each of which helps him gain control in the conversation in which he is engaged since Don García is a master of manipulating language either to deceive blatantly or to *engañar con la verdad* [deceive with the truth]. The quintessential characteristics of these new identities are the frequency of their appearance and the manner in which the character names himself. García moves freely from one identity to another, often establishing each new role by affirming, "Yo soy *X*" [I am *X*]. He baptizes himself anew countless times; yet, because of sheer repetition and inherent contradictions—and because of the contrast between oral and written discourse—the force of this process of naming is gradually weakened until, like his other words, even García's names for himself become suspect.

The institution of naming in *La verdad sospechosa* is complex. Baptism functions on two distinct levels that are brought closer together in the course of the play. The first level deals with identification by means of the assigning of a proper name. By insisting upon identifying his beautiful "mystery woman" as "Lucrecia," García loses the woman he loves, since his innocent error in incorrectly identifying (in misnaming) Jacinta leads, as many critics have noted, to the play's dénouement.[3] The second level, the metaphoric baptisms that García uses to define himself, may be categorized by type. Some of these social self-definitions appear as simple, generic descriptions; several reflect his own changing perceptions of himself in the course of the play. In fact, there are so many of these descriptions that their number becomes unwieldy, and Don García eventually begins to lose control over them. The various self-definitions that he has created become troublesome for García precisely because they are mutually exclusive. Still others are outright lies. In these cases, Don García gets caught in his own linguistic trap because other characters begin to doubt the truth of all of his names or self-definitions, as well as his intentions in other areas.

The question, then, is how to relate the two broad categories of generic and proper names, or of self-definition and identification, as they appear throughout the play.[4] Whether a name is used on the literal level of a proper name or as a kind of metaphoric process of defining through a large number of social categories, in *La verdad sospechosa* the institution of naming relates to language's ability to identify, describe, and make real. Names on both levels lead to the same kind of verbal legitimization. They function in order to make real the person so described; the name *counts as*[5] the person or quality expressed in the formulas "Yo soy *X*" [I am *X*] and "Ella es *X*" [She is *X*]. Thus, the process of legitimizing through real or metaphorical, successful or unsuccessful baptisms links García's misnaming of Jacinta to his own assumptions of multiple identities.

García's frequent acts of naming relate directly to the ways that speakers use words as a means to gain control in social discourse. Throughout most of the play, language serves García well as a medium for exerting control and attaining power. Upon occasion, however, speakers find that their own words can also undercut their control, reliability, or authority. Don García is Alarcón's ironic example *par excellence* of a speaker who suffers because he loses control over the power of language. As the protagonist plays with names—and subsequently with the truth—he finds that language, his weapon for attacking the structure of the social hierarchy and for achieving his own ends, becomes a self-defeating tool as well. Language, then, subverts García's controlling role in the same situations he has been trying to manipulate. The names that García uses highlight this ironic use of words and serve as useful indices of the linguistic complexity of Alarcón's play.

One way in which Don García plays with both truth and language in order to gain control and power for himself involves his rebellion against his father and against society in general. In this way, he seeks a definition of himself that will render him distinct from the rest of the world:

> Quien vive sin ser sentido,
> quien sólo el número aumenta
> y haze lo que todos hazen,
> ¿en qué difiere de bestia?
> Ser famosos es gran cosa,
> el medio qual fuere sea.
> Nómbrenme a mí en todas partes,
> y murmúrenme siquiera;

[He who lives without being noticed, / he who only serves to increase the numbers / and does what everybody else does, / how is he different from a beast? / It's a great thing to be famous / no matter how. / Let people speak my name everywhere / even if it is among rumors of disapproval.]

(1.8.857–64)

That others would talk about him is obviously not García's worry. Instead, he begs to be identified, to gain notoriety with no regard to the means employed. In order to achieve the fame he desires, he uses language to transform his world, for García believes in the primacy of the word, and he proves himself a master of artistic creation through his lies.[6] He sets himself up as opposing the philosophy of his father, who declares that lying is without purpose and is ignoble in a noble man. Don García reveals himself to be extremely self-conscious in using words to undercut the authority of his father: "¡Qué fácil de persuadir / quien tiene amor suele ser! / ¡Y qué fácil en creer / el que no sabe mentir!" [How easy it is to persuade / those who are full of love for us! / And how easily / those who do not know how to lie believe] (2.10.1744–47). As the play progresses, García's lies include the act of self-consciously adopting a succession of roles, of explicitly defining himself as multiple characters, some of whom even simultaneously oppose each other.[7]

García's role playing suggests rich representational possibilities, since, as Richard Hornby reminds us, "role playing within the role is an excellent means for delineating character, by showing not only who the character is, but what he wants to be" (*Drama, Metadrama, and Perception* 67). As the play opens, we are presented with García, the student from Salamanca. This is the only major identity that is revealed solely through García's costume and the comments of other characters. Yet García's identity as a student carries with it a wealth of connotative information. While a student, García has been a part of the world of youthful tricks, game-playing, and deception:

Letrado. En Salamanca, Señor,
son moços, gastan humor,
sigue cada qual su gusto;
hazen donayre del vicio,
gala de la travessura,
grandeza de la locura:
haze, al fin, la edad su oficio.

[*Graduate-Tutor.* In Salamanca, sir, / they are young, they are full of humorous intent; / each one does whatever pleases him; / vice is funny to them, / pranks are their pride / all forms of craziness are acts of greatness for them: / after all, these are the hallmarks of youth.]
(1.2.170–76)

The Letrado's description of "moços" [youths] associates Don García with youthful pranks and with a disregard for moral norms. Furthermore, García's studies and mentor have a direct bearing on his formation: García has been studying with the

Letrado, which implies training in rhetoric and an introduction to the power of language. Don García thus seems amply prepared for the type of linguistic deception he will practice upon arriving in Madrid. The Letrado's comments and the young man's clothing help to define Don García as an educated, but mischievous, youth, one whose training and experience have given him a basic introduction to the ways that language can be used as a tool for gaining control in society.

García's own explicit attempt at self-definition, however, would seem to contradict this initial presentation of the protagonist as a precocious prankster when he answers Tristán's question, "¿Eres tierno?" ["are you tender-hearted?" but also "are you a green horn?"] with "Moço soy" [I am young]. Here, García seemingly admits his innocence in the ways of the court—and of women—to his new mentor, Tristán. García uses the identity of "moço" to describe a different, more naive aspect of his character. He presents himself as eager to learn, and he is given an opportune lesson in the type of deception practiced in Madrid society. Tristán instructs García in the value of appearance, to be repeated in later "lessons" (such as "Dissimula y ten paciencia" [Dissimulate, and be patient]) that ironically contrast with his sententious moralizing on the vice of lying.

Don García, then, proffers two apparently contradictory definitions of "moço" in the early part of the play. If García is feigning ignorance (based on his earlier preparation for deceit learned in Salamanca), he establishes himself as completely deceptive from the outset of the play. The first two definitions that he assigns himself (through dress and self-description) thus display the mutually exclusive opposition of street-smart student versus naive youth. If he is not dissembling, it may be because the type of deception that he learned earlier (in his Salamanca experiences) was not the same type that he encounters in Madrid: that of the big city, court intrigue, and the world of women. His education is now stengthened by the addition of this new information on deception. In this case, the two examples are not mutually exclusive and become two more generic self-descriptions, two of many more to follow. Both options are plausible. In either case, or in both, García's first blatant self-description as "moço" may be viewed as an example of deceiving with the truth, as the young man with the checkered past enters a new level of deception in the society of Madrid.

Don García's description as "moço" thereby ironically establishes him as a typical student, a naive youth, and as a deceiving rake from the outset of the play. Yet he adopts another role almost immediately, as part of his first patently obvious lie. Upon meeting Jacinta, who has fallen, García offers her his hand, describing himself metaphorically:

> Esta mano
> os servid de que os levante,
> si merezco ser Atlante
> de un cielo tan soberano.

[Let this hand / help you rise, / if I may be described as the Atlas / of such a sovereign heaven.]

(1.4.437–40)

His self-definition as Atlas is accepted by Jacinta as the typical hyperbolic language of Golden Age *galanes* [male lovers], and the two subsequently engage in a brief scene of wordplay. Then and only then does Don García change his tactics from hyperbolic metaphor to outright lie, telling Jacinta that when he arrived from the "indiano suelo" [Indian soil], she was the first person he saw. Don García's words indicate that he has come from the Spanish American colonies, the Indies; the implication is that he is extremely wealthy. He further affirms that he has been following her secretly for a year. The exchange below illuminates García's technique:

> *Jacinta.* ¿Soys indiano?
> *García.* Y tales son
> mis riquezas, pues os vi,
> que al minado Potosí
> le quito la presunción.

[*Jacinta.* Do you come from the Indies? / *García.* And my wealth is such that, since I saw you, / I now surpass mine-rich Potosí itself.]

(1.5.497–500)

García does not answer Jacinta's question directly, but he does imply an affirmative response to her question. He reveals an acute awareness of the power of language to transform the world, taking advantage of the well-known tactic of implying, rather than explicitly stating, that something is the case, and letting the listener fill in the gaps with words she wants to hear. His desire to impress Jacinta is reflected in the adoption of a self-definition that suggests wealth and exotic mystique. García's implications, metaphoric language, and blatant untruths serve as his media for assuming control in the relationship.

García's self-definition as *indiano* is directly related to both the next scene and the ending of the play. Having fallen instantly in love, García tries to find out the name of the beautiful young woman he saw—although two women are standing next to each other. Tristán details a coachman's words: that the more beautiful woman of the two is named Doña Lucrecia de Luna. Language obfuscates the situation in this relatively early scene, since García's insistence upon naming Jacinta leads to the error that ultimately causes him to lose her. García insists upon assigning a proper name to this "mystery woman," with the result that he misnames or misidentifies her. This is an innocent error, based on varying perceptions of beauty, yet it is legitimized by the act of naming, of verbally fixing an identity. There is, then, a parallel between this error in misnaming and the generic definitions (some of which are misnames and/or lies) that García ascribes to himself. Although different in origin, both lead to a similar verbal legitimization, reflecting the power of a name (here, in its dual aspects of identification and social definition) to make real, to signify its referent accurately.

The conflict between differing views of social definition and the authority of one's name is perhaps best illustrated by the following conversation between Don García and his father, Don Beltrán, an exchange that underscores the definition of a gentleman:

D. Beltrán. ¿Soys cavallero, García?
D. García. Téngome por hijo vuestro.
D. Beltrán. ¿Y basta ser hijo mío
para ser vos cavallero?
D. García. Yo pienso, señor, que sí.

[*D. Beltrán.* Are you a noble gentleman, García? / *D. García.* I am your son, after all. / *D. Beltrán.* And is your being my son / enough for you to be considered a noble gentleman? / *D. García.* I think it is, sir.]
(2.9.1396–1400)

Don Beltrán argues that a *caballero* expresses nobility and achieves a good reputation through noble actions.[8] Notwithstanding his own questionable act of trying to get his son quickly married before society finds out that García is a liar, Don Beltrán represents social authority of a more traditional order. Don Beltrán's philosophy is opposed, however, by Don García's view: that nobility is innate, the result of noble lineage. Don García operates based on this second interpretation of the noun *caballero* in describing himself and his role in society. He considers himself a noble gentleman, and although he does not always reflect his father's interpretation of the word, he does frequently act in accordance with his own self-definition.

Yet, for García, this definition of a *caballero* is not wholly tied to the question of noble lineage. As the play progresses, García occasionally *acts* as a noble man, gradually altering his actions to reflect more nearly the definition of Don Beltrán. When García and his rival, Don Juan de Sosa, meet on the field of honor, Don García cannot walk away after being challenged:

> me obligastes, y es forçoso,
> puesto que tengo de hazer
> como quien soy, no bolver
> sino muerto o vitorioso.
>
> [you made me respond to my obligation, and it cannot be otherwise; / since I have to act / in accordance with who I am, / I must return either dead or victorious.]
>
> (2.11.1812–15)

"Como quien soy" [in accordance with who I am] functions as a formulaic metaphor for the innate role that García assumes within his society, which is governed by the honor code. When it comes to the question of bravery, of responding to a challenge to his own definition of honor, Don García both names himself and acts as a *caballero*.

Nevertheless, even by referring to himself as a *caballero,* García also simultaneously illustrates how naming can obfuscate meaning and deceive listeners. At the duel, he uses another lie to persuade Don Juan that Jacinta did not attend his mythical banquet: García affirms that his guest was a married woman who had just arrived in Madrid. He attempts to legitimize this lie by declaring, "de no verla más os doy / palabra, como quien soy, / o quedar por fementido" [I give you my word / that I shall not see her again, / in accordance with who I am; / otherwise, I will have to answer for my breach of promise] (2.11.1801–3). Don García links his self-definition as a *caballero* (again, with the words "como quien soy") to a lie, a description of a nonexistent woman, and he does so while standing on the field of honor. By infusing a lie into the duel itself, García undermines the authority of the honor code because he consciously manipulates language and his status as a noble speaker in order to take advantage of the static, rule-governed code for duelling, a code ultimately governed by the conventions of the honor code. He cleverly attempts to make his lies acceptable by affirming his identity within the system of honor, a system of noble actions and noble language. The name that Don García gives himself, *caballero,* thus ironically loses its power at the very moment that he is trying to act nobly by defending his own impugned honor, *precisely* because of the way that García's words undercut his actions.[9]

These two contradictory uses of the identity of *caballero* are reflected in the utterance "como quien soy," a formula that offers a key example of how language is used to convey multiple levels of meaning in *La verdad sospechosa.* Don Juan de Sosa has known Don García since their days as students in Salamanca. Therefore, he not only has the background to know about García's personality, but he also knew him in the context of his lying and trickery as a student. It is consequently logical to assume that Don Juan would—or should—know that although Don García swears that something is true, his reputation as a liar should make the statement suspect. In fact, it is fair to state that Don Juan should assume that when García swears as "como quien soy," he is ironically defining himself as both a *caballero* and a liar.

Don García is boldly called a "mentiroso" [liar], "embarrador" [deceitful], and "embustero" [a teller of lies] by other characters many times in the course of *La verdad sospechosa.* In his soliloquy, he explicitly defines himself as a liar in response to his father's reprimand: "¡Bueno fue reñir conmigo / porque en quanto digo miento" [A lot of good it does to scold me, / because everything I say is a lie.] (2.10.1740–41). This self-description, where García proudly boasts that he is a liar, displays his conscious delight in deceiving his father. In this soliloquy, García functions as both the speaker and listener of his utterance. He pleases himself, and he glories in the self-gratification expressed earlier: "al fin, es éste mi gusto, / que es la razón de más fuerça" [after all, this is what I want, / which is the strongest motivation of all for what I do] (1.8.867–68).

We have seen García describe himself as a student, youth, a metaphoric Atlas, *indiano,* famous person, noble/gentleman, and liar. Each new identity that García assumes leads us to a greater awareness of his character as he tries to assert his authority through language. Each new name, however, also functions cumulatively to weaken the effect of succeeding names; as he assumes multiple, often conflicting roles, Don García's words begin to lose authority through sheer repetition. This loss of authority is precisely what results from his next series of identities, that of the lover or suitor of "Lucrecia," who is, of course, Jacinta.

As the ardent suitor of the woman whom he believes is named Lucrecia, Don García learns the value of telling the truth. It is certainly as Jacinta's suitor that he becomes trapped in his lies. Ironically, the more he tries to explain the truth, the more his words are considered suspect by the women. As we will soon discuss in greater detail, in an effort to get "Lucrecia" to believe that he loves only her, that he is not really married, García truthfully describes himself, proclaiming on four different occasions that he is single, a bachelor. The act of asserting this definition so many times represents an attempt to get "Lucrecia" to equate the truth with the insistent repetition of his words. García essentially affirms, "I am who I say I am, and therefore you must believe me." This is an outgrowth of his earlier identification with the stock phrase "como quien soy," the basis of the whole honor system, which precludes lying. Again, dramatic irony offers the key to explain García's apparent use of his status as a noble speaker to support his claims and to manipulate the system in order to satisfy his desires.

García's most poetic example of self-definition presents the literate *galán* [male lover] consciously assuming his role:

D. García. ¿Es Lucrecia?
Lucrecia. ¿Es Don García?
D. García. Es quien oy la joya halló
más preciosa que labró
el Cielo en la Platería;
es quien, en llegando a vella,
tanto estimó su valor,
que dio, abrasado de amor,
la vida y alma por ella.
Soy, al fin, el que precia
de ser vuestro, y soy quien oy
comienço a ser, porque soy
el esclavo de Lucrecia.

[*García.* Is that Lucrecia? / *Lucrecia.* Is that Don García? / *García.* It is the one who found today / the most precious gem / ever cut by any silversmith in Heaven; / it is the one who, upon seeing her, / found her of such value / that, searing with love, he gave / his life and his soul in exchange for her. / I am, in conclusion, the one who most wants / to be yours; and as of today I am / born anew, because I am / Lucrecia's slave.]

(2.16.1960–71)

Although Don García speaks metaphorically of his beloved in terms of her commercial value, his definition of himself is, quite literally, apt: "soy quien oy / comienço a ser" [as of today I am / born anew]. García has consciously changed his self-definition to include a new focus, a new reason for being. His metaphoric role as Lucrecia's slave reflects his commitment to serve the woman he loves from that moment on.

Yet, to win the hand of his beloved, García must posit even more identities. All of these new definitions revolve around the pairing of *soltero* [single] and *casado* [married]. The first time he claims to be a married man, García lies:

D. García. Entristézcome porque es
imposible obedeceros.
D. Beltrán. ¿Por qué?
D. García. Porque soy casado.

[*D. García.* I am sad because / it is impossible for me to obey you. / *D. Beltrán.* But why? / *D. García.* Because I am already married.]
(2.9.1510–12)

In this instance, Don García assumes the role of a married man to forestall his father's plans to marry him to a woman he assumes he does not know. After achieving success with that ploy, he varies the theme in a number of scenes with "Lucrecia." He repeatedly swears that he is single—or, at least, single as far as she is concerned:

Soltero soy, vive Dios.

[I am single, by God!]
(2.16.1986)

Vive Dios, que soy soltero.

[By God, I am single.]
(2.16.1991)

mientras hazer espero
con vuestra mano mis bodas,
soy casado para todas
sólo para vos soltero.

[while I hope / to take your hand when we get married, / I am married when it concerns all other women / but for you alone I am single.]
(2.16.2044–47)

Y buelvo a jurar, por Dios,
que, en este amoroso estado,
para todas soy casado,
y soltero para vos.

[And I swear it again, by God, / that, in this state of love, / I am married as far as all women are concerned / but I am single for you.] (3.6.2526–29)

García repeatedly identifies himself as a bachelor in order to gain "Lucrecia's" affection. He bases the argument of his protestations of love on the fact that he is the person he claims to be. Ironically, his tactic misfires, either because his listeners are laboring under false assumptions, or because they have seen him lie too many times before. Jacinta exemplifies the response of García's listeners: "Que la boca mentirosa / incurre en tan torpe mengua, / que, solamente en su lengua, / es la verdad sospechosa" [a mouth that only tells lies / is so defective / that truth itself becomes suspect / if it is uttered by its tongue] (3.6.2626–29).

García also seeks to legitimize his spoken words with a declaration in writing. Acknowledging that the spoken word alone has proven insufficient to convince "Lucrecia," he confirms his love by means of a written vow:

Ya que mal crédito cobras
de mis palabras sentidas
dime si serán creídas,
pues nunca mienten las obras.
Que si consiste el creerme,
señora, en ser tu marido,
y ha de dar el ser creído
materia al favorecerme,
por éste, Lucrecia mía,
que de mi mano te doy
firmado, digo que soy
ya tu esposo Don García.

[If my sincere words / deserve so little credit, / tell me if my actions / will be believed: actions do not lie. / For if you will only believe me / if I am your husband, / and if I need something tangible / to make you start believing me, / by means of this document, my dear Lucrecia, / signed by the hand that I give you / I proclaim that I am now your husband Don García.]

(3.6.2448–59)

This letter is of fundamental importance to the play, since it signals a decisive turn in Don García's character development. The youth who scorned the value of noble deeds and actions now claims that "nunca mienten las obras" [actions never lie]. In this scene, García has come full circle to proclaim the value of acting over speaking. He knew that language could constitute authority and give him power and fame; he now acknowledges that the spoken word can also subvert his own authority. The *mentiroso* [liar] is not totally reformed, but he *has* exhibited a dramatic change in character development. It is thus fitting that he uses a written text to explain and strengthen his position: García has learned to distrust the spoken word. The power of speech in tranforming reality has become suspect, even to a skillful liar. He therefore attempts to make his case even more acceptable, more convincing, by means of naming himself in writing: "soy / ya tu esposo Don García" [I am / now your husband Don García].

Unfortunately for García, the letter is delivered to Lucrecia, and not Jacinta. Since the recipient ("wife of Don García") is not spelled out, the letter becomes a potentially dangerous object in terms of the actions at the play's end. This letter incarnates the ultimate act of naming, because it is legitimized by writing, and because it leads to García's marriage to the "wrong" woman at the conclusion of the play. The letter makes explicit the contrast between the value of the written word (a contract forged on paper) and the spoken words of a noble-born character (one who has both rights and responsibilities within the system supported by the honor code) in this seventeenth-century play.

La verdad sospechosa is a play about the power of language and about how words can undermine—and be undermined by—speakers who use words to exert control. Yet it is also about how language creates worlds through naming. García uses language to undermine more traditional forms of authority and simultaneously to raise himself to a position of power and fame; this use of language is tied to his constant attempts to define himself socially. He bases the truth of what he says on his own self-definition, a definition that is in a constant process of change. Still, just as the sheer number of other lies that García tells gradually causes other characters to doubt him when he does speak the truth, so, too, do the multiplicity and types of names that García ascribes to himself eventually weaken the definition of the protagonist and cause him to lose authority and control as a speaker. This is due, in part, to the fact that many of García's assumed roles are either blatant lies *(indiano)* or mutually exclusive identities (liar *and* nobleman, bachelor *and* husband). Furthermore, we must question García's sincerity in asserting to his father that he is married to Doña Sancha, or in describing himself as a rich *indiano* to Jacinta. García's word is thus not always his bond.[10]

It is also the overwhelming number of names that ultimately lessens their validity. In assigning himself so many different names, these multiple linguistic signs *(moço, estudiante, indiano, caballero, mentiroso, Atlante, soltero, esposo/casado)* [a young man, a student, a rich man returned from the Indies, a nobleman, a liar, Atlas, a bachelor, a husband/married man] point toward the same referent. It must be noted here that a number of nonconflicting identities may be used appropriately—even at the same time. García can be a student, *moço,* nobleman, and bachelor simultaneously; thus, several of his self-definitions accurately reflect various aspects of his character. The problem is one of asserting—or here losing—control through the assumption of so many self-definitions.[11] García expresses this view himself, noting the link between naming and defining his character: "no soy dueño / de mí mismo" [I am not the master / of my own self] (1.8.797–98).

The identities that García assumes are, again, ironically tied to his loss of the woman he wants to marry. His emphasis on naming, on basing Jacinta's identity on a single linguistic sign (an emphasis that opposes García's own self-referential baptisms), leads him to err in incorrectly identifying the woman he loves. He steadfastly maintains that the name *is* the woman, and he loses her as a result. Thus, García's insistent misnaming of Lucrecia/Jacinta offers a counterpoint to his own attempts to define himself through a large number of social categories. In both the case of García's names for himself and in that of his misnaming Jacinta, the power of language to define/describe the world becomes suspect, and it becomes suspect precisely because it is ironically undercut by other words and other names.

Linguistic conventions assume a speaker's willingness to communicate appropriately and sincerely. The notion of sincerity in the pairing of *caballero* [a nobleman] and *mentiroso* [a liar] in Don García's self-depiction is particularly salient. Don García's definition for the word *caballero* would seem to deny the Golden Age view (represented by Don Beltrán) that a liar cannot also be noble. The honor code was firmly grounded in the unity of noble actions and noble language; indeed, language as an act, a form of overt behavior, necessarily falls within the realm of noble actions.

Consequently, it would appear that Don García does not use language to communicate sincerely and that, on the contrary, his verbal behavior undermines linguistic and social conventions for appropriate language use by noble speakers. Yet the lessons that García has learned from his first moments in Madrid reflect an ironic definition of the court as simultaneously noble and deceptive. Tristán describes the members of the court (and particularly its women) in terms of deceptive appearance versus reality. Don Beltrán echoes this view and acts upon it in his haste to get García married before society finds out that his son is a liar. Jacinta and Lucrecia overtly use deception and role reversal as a kind of game that they play with García. Consequently, García is not the only character who acts—and speaks—inappropriately or insincerely. He defines himself as both a liar and a *caballero* because that definition is in practice, if not in theory, accurate—both on a personal level, and in society as a whole. The other roles he assumes thus reflect the social acceptability of simultaneously adopting multiple identities in referring to himself.

Seen together as a unit, García's acts of discourse, including the assumption of a multiplicity of identities, underscore the perception of the world he encounters in Madrid and illustrate the union of García's past world of the university with his present world of the court. The common denominators in this union appear to be deception and games-playing—particularly with words. García assimilates the lessons he has learned about Madrid and applies them to his new world each time he speaks. Societal forces influence his speech, and García's changing descriptions of himself reflect this. Don García thus simultaneously mirrors and creates worlds out of the words he uses to describe and identify himself. His linguistic behavior apes the conventions of Madrid society, thereby calling attention to the deception practiced at court and leading us to uncover an underlying social critique.[12]

Yet if Don García's lies are merely an exaggeration of the games of deception he has learned to master in Madrid—and for which he had been prepared by his studies in Salamanca—we must still discover why he alone is punished at the end of the play. The obvious answers are that he has been caught in too many lies (including many of the names that he ascribes to himself), or that his lies are more frequent and/or more serious than those of other characters—views that are supported by the text. These readings can be amplified by returning again to two key points developed in this study. First, the idea that Don García constantly plays with language as a tool for establishing identity makes possible his misnaming of Jacinta: that fact leads irrevocably to his pursuit of the wrong woman. Both with reference to Jacinta and in terms of his own baptisms, García places too much faith on language's power to make real and to create, rather than merely point toward reality. The irony of the play, however, is that García gradually—and belatedly—learns that the spoken word can *also* cause misunderstandings. García's refusal to comprehend fully the inherent ambiguity and indeterminacy of language leads to the protagonist's undoing. This leads us to the second explanation for Don García's punishment through marriage to a woman he does not love: García pledges his faith—and seals his fate—in a written contract of love and marriage, a contract that becomes binding by virtue of having Don García's name signed at the end. The fact that García's honor has been sealed in writing ultimately leaves him no choice in marriage. The written contract formalizes his spoken pledges of love, and García becomes a victim not only of speech, but also of writing. His world therefore becomes defined and bound by his acts of written and oral discourse.[13]

Yet, our discussion of Don García's multiple self-definitions should not end on a negative note. The creativity that his discourse displays relates to a number of philosophical questions regarding the nature of human identity and the status of the linguistic sign. In *The Order of Things,* Michel Foucault describes the early half of the seventeenth century as the period initiating a complete alteration in the organization of signs: "On the threshold of the Classical age, the sign ceases to be a form of the world; and it ceases to be bound to what it marks by the solid and secret bonds of resemblance or affinity" (58). This idea suggests a number of implications for our discussion of *La verdad sospechosa,* which was written in 1619. Following Foucault's argument, a more conservative view of Don García's self-definitions would posit the idea that the various signs that refer to the protagonist establish a kind of one-to-one correspondence between the sign and the referent. Don Beltrán, for example, would represent that view by insisting that the word *caballero* [noble gentleman] defines a person who *is* noble, and who *acts* nobly. A seventeenth-century perspective, however, would deny such a conclusion: "the sign does not wait in silence for the coming of a man capable of recognizing it" (59). This seventeenth-century perspective seems to reflect more accurately Don García's view of the world. Don García, a specialist in creative verbal behavior, tests the limits of the sign and builds new realities out of language. His own prior understanding of who he is leads him to seek words that will match this identity. García's multiple self-definitions, then, create a characterization that underscores not only the differences between himself and his father, but between the sixteenth and the seventeenth centuries. The generational battle thus duplicates the conflictive relationship existing between the changing ages and between signs and referents, words and things, language and reality.

In her call for more "seriously critical linguistics," Mary Louise Pratt makes an observation that directly relates to *La verdad sospechosa* and the union of worlds and words:

> representative discourse is always engaged in both fitting words to world and fitting world to words; language and linguistic insitutions in part construct or constitute the world for people in speech communities, rather than merely depicting it. We need to think of all representative discourses, fictional or non-fictional, as simultaneously world-describing and world-changing undertakings. ("Ideology" 16)

Pratt's comments can help us unravel the ways that García uses language in *La verdad sospechosa* and explore their application to our own linguistic worlds. Don García may place too much faith in the power of words, and he may not fully comprehend the ways that language—in both oral and written discourse—can alter, as well as reflect, reality, but he nevertheless brings a creative quality, a dynamic style to the community of speakers he has joined. Consequently, by examining the protagonist's verbal action, by analyzing how he refers to himself and to his social reality, we can see how literal and metaphoric discourse tests the limits of the society depicted in this Alarcón play, which may then allow us to relate the lessons we learn about the nature of language to our own linguistic communities.

4

Language Games in the Theater: The Case of *El caballero de Olmedo*

Your questions refer to words; so I must speak about words.
—Ludwig Wittgenstein

In the preceding analysis, we saw how games played with language are tied to contexts, at times overlapping, but contexts in which the essential rules for acceptable linguistic use are subject to variation. In *La verdad sospechosa,* Don García failed to make all of the adjustments necessary to express himself felicitously within his particular linguistic community, and he was consequently frustrated. We will examine the kinds of discourse at work in Lope's *El caballero de Olmedo* [*The Knight from Olmedo*] from a different but complementary perspective, utilizing a number of Ludwig Wittgenstein's important contributions to language philosophy as part of the implicit superstructure of our analysis. Wittgenstein's contributions, however, will be filtered through those of another critic, Keir Elam, a semiotician of the theater who has appropriated Wittgenstein's notion of the language game to describe the dynamics of the theatrical experience in an insightful study, *Shakespeare's Universe of Discourse.* Elam's study is particularly well suited to our own analysis of *El caballero de Olmedo* because it successfully extends Wittgenstein's view of the language game to cover the kinds of linguistic transactions that occur specifically in the theater. Consequently, because of its specificity in a dramatic context and because of its own cohesiveness, Elam's approach serves as the theoretical guide for our discussion of Lope's *El caballero de Olmedo.*

Elam's study describes Wittgenstein's view of the language game, that is, language in action, as the quintessential metaphor for the role of discourse in the theater and in dramatic texts.[1] The fundamental point of Wittgenstein's approach to language is that it is best studied from the pragmatic perspective of language in use. Language, then, is not an abstract system, but rather a working, functional method of communication: when we speak, we act. Elam refines this idea to present his own definition of the language game, which is "any distinct form of language use subject to its own rules and defined within a given behavioural context" (10–11). Thus, language games do not necessarily have ludic qualities, nor do they have anything to do with witty repartée; rather, they show use within contextual parameters in a pragmatic focus on the union of words and their contexts.

Elam observes that discourse in the theater is an especially rich area for exploring language games precisely because dramatic discourse "is always destined, if not on the page then at least potentially on the stage, to interact with its physical and behavioural surroundings, and especially with the body and its movements, in the production of meaning" (12). He selects Wittgenstein's notion of the language game as his theoretical model "because of its flexibility and multiformity, because of its mixed semiotic status, because of its dependence on a physical and behavioural context" (12).

This suggests that dramatic discourse involves multiple levels of communication and interpretation. On a most basic level, we know that dramatists seek to communicate with their audiences via the dialogue their characters utter, although those dramatists depend upon a number of other agents (producers, directors, actors) to assist in representing those words by contextualizing them actively. We are also reminded, however, that discourse in a play is always directly linked to physical levels of communication and that in the theater words and actions combine to create a unified and dynamic experience. These comments regarding the multileveled nature of communication in the theater may not be revolutionary, but they do allow us to emphasize the point that Elam's reading of Wittgenstein, as well as our own reading of both the literary critic and the philosopher, are based on the value of seeing dramatic discourse as inherently active. This is, of course, remarkably similar to J. L. Austin's view of the links between speech and action, which were examined in the early chapters of this book.

Elam's study of Shakespeare's comedies presents five general categories of language games. The first category, **theatrical games,** has to do with putting performances on stage within the drama. Theatrical games deal with indicating or describing objects, using and referring to stage properties, etc. The second category, that of **world-creating games,** concerns deixis (defining the protagonist and context of the dramatic situation, *Semiotics* 72), exposition, and reference within the possible world created onstage. **Semantic games** describe the relationships between signs, while **pragmatic games** pertain to the realities of language in use, such as issues of sincerity and appropriateness in speaking, turn-taking, etc. Finally, the fifth category, that of **figural games,** has to do with the nonliteral links between saying and doing, including such tropes and figures as repetition, irony, hyperbole, metaphor, and metonymy, and the use of proverbs or neologisms. Elam notes that these five types of language games are "levels *activated* in the plays as specific dramatic and comic doings rather than remaining inert elements of verbal structure" (17). The dramatic discourse of all plays contains multiple examples of these five kinds of language games, but different plays contain different numbers or emphasize different types.

Elam views Shakespeare's comedies as being highly self-conscious in their language use. Consequently he describes Shakespeare's foregrounding of the language games found in the comedies in terms of frames placed around the games. These five categories of language games are activated precisely because they are presented in a self-conscious manner. Metalanguage and metadiscourse illustrate language in use because our attention is drawn to the verbal action of the plays in question in which language is seen as object.[2] The characters' direct references to language, naming, meaning, dramatic communication, reference, and the like all serve to frame the dialogue spoken by those characters. As the characters speak, they perform a double function: they act with words in order to *re-act* to the present dramatic situation and to underscore the entire idea that language is an active, living phenomenon. In this manner, Elam concludes that the game-frame dialectic exploits language as activity and as object, lending Shakespearean comedy much of its discursive momentum and depth (21).

The preceding discussion suggests, however, that Elam's five basic types of language games display the kinds of linguistic experiences that occur in all types of dramatic genres. Elam utilizes the concept of the language game and its complementary frame to examine comedy, but his analysis ultimately emerges as a useful model for discussing language-as-action from the perspective of other dramatic contexts as well. The fact that his theories are not intrinsically tied to comedy therefore increases the likelihood that they may prove equally useful for analyzing the *comedia,* which combined tragedy with comedy. Even more specifically, it suggests that Elam's ideas will work well with *El caballero de Olmedo,* which maintains a comic structure throughout most of the play, only to metamorphose into a tragedy at the drama's end.

Wittgenstein's view of language as action, appropriated by Elam as the interplay of games and frames in Shakespeare's comedies, is, then, a viable springboard for the study of language in Lope's highly controversial play, *El caballero de Olmedo.* As we will see, this interplay of games and frames defines *El caballero*'s structure. The types of language games that Elam describes as being particularly conspicuous in Shakespeare are equally central to the development of Lope's drama; moreover, the self-conscious framing of those games highlights them, marking them so that we can understand better the essence of this Golden Age text.

In 1972, Bruce Wardropper noted that although "Lope's plays thwart systematic critical procedures," at least a few "critical breakthroughs have occurred" ("The Criticism of the Spanish *Comedia*" 178). Wardropper viewed *Fuenteovejuna* as a play that was finally receiving the kind of critical attention that it merited, and he further suggested that *El caballero de Olmedo* would soon follow as one of the few Lopean dramas that really would be understood well. Indeed, the play received a great deal of critical interest from the mid-1960s to the mid-1970s. J. W. Sage proposes, perhaps a bit overzealously, that "no Golden Age play has caused more disagreement among commentators of Spanish literature" than *El caballero de Olmedo* (*Lope de Vega: El caballero de Olmedo* 9). That disagreement has been seen in such far-ranging issues as Lope's use of certain literary and extraliterary sources in the play, the structural conflict between the comic trajectory of the first two acts and the tragedy of act 3, the interpretation of the drama's rich symbols and images from the perspective of Christian redemption, and the entire notion of poetic justice à la A. A. Parker, which posits the idea that the guilty must suffer the consequences of their actions and that the innocent will not be punished.

The drama begins as a conventional *comedia de capa y espada* [cloak and sword comedy], in which Don Alonso, the knight of Olmedo, and Doña Inés, from Medina, fall in love and, with the help of a Celestinesque go-between, Fabia,[3] attempt to forestall Inés's father's plans to marry her to one Don Rodrigo. The love interest and comic aspects seen in the first two acts are replaced, however, with a much more tragic final act, culminating in the presaged death of Don Alonso, who is murdered late at night while on the road between Medina and Olmedo. Although Don Rodrigo and the other perpetrators of this murder are apprehended and brought to justice, the lovers are nevertheless separated forever. We are only promised that the memory of Don Alonso will live on:

en las lenguas de la fama
a quien conserven respeto
la mudanza de los hombres
y los olvidos del tiempo.

[in the tongues of Fame, / respected / by the metamorphoses that men go through / and by the oblivion of time.]

(3.2705–8)

This study offers examples of the types of language games seen in *El caballero de Olmedo* by showing how those games are framed through such techniques as heightening, suspension, and connotation, and finally by indicating the ways that Lope has "placed language—structurally, thematically, and theatrically—*en abyme*" in Gide's sense that theatrical texts frequently emerge as self-mirroring metatexts (Elam 23).

Theatrical games indicate or describe objects, use or refer to stage props, or even deal with metadramatic techniques. The theatrical game emphasizes the "relationship of language to theatrical activity: the physical, vocal, gestural, and scenic conditions of . . . stage activity" (Elam 12). Lope's play employs a great number of such games because so many levels of theater are at work in *El caballero de Olmedo.* For example, in an early comic scene, the cowardly *gracioso,* Tello, has been asked to help the Celestinesque Fabia steal a tooth from a hanged highwayman. This scene first presents a theatrical game, focusing on objects and stage properties, as the *gracioso* tells his master that he will need a ladder and pliers to "sacar una dama de su casa" [abduct a lady from her house] (1.672). The game, however, is also figural, using metaphor and irony, and is therefore framed in a highly self-conscious manner. Don Alonso, who does not know about the referent of "sacar una dama de su casa," counsels his servant:

Mira lo que haces, Tello;
no entres adonde no salgas.

[Be careful in what you are doing, Tello / and don't go in where you may not come out.]

(1.673–74)

Don Alonso has assumed that the *dama* in question is a *doncella* [young girl] rather than a tooth; this misconception proffers a metaphoric parallel to his own future efforts to liberate Doña Inés from her father's control. Even more ironic, however, is his advice that Tello be careful not to enter a place from which there is no escape. Had Don Alonso heeded his own words of counsel, he might not have died on the road between Medina and Olmedo.

Other examples of theatrical games abound in *El caballero de Olmedo*. The play contains numerous allusions to clothing, a subject that has been explored by several critics.[4] Don Alonso's description of Inés's shoes, her use of a ribbon to signal her lover, the cape appropriated by Tello, Fabia's use of laundry as a ploy that allows her to escape detection and to come and go freely from the house, and Tello's disguise as a student are all among the props and costumes alluded to continually by the other characters. The sheer number of references to outward appearance and disguise reveals the self-conscious nature of the theatrical games that involve references to clothing. Appearance and reality merge in such self-reflexive scenes as the one in which Fabia and Tello arrive disguised as the holy woman and Latin teacher who will help to "instruct" Inés in the ways of the church. In reality, though, they plan to teach her about secular love and to serve as her go-betweens with Don Alonso.

That play within the play is a framed language game that delights in its self-consciousness. Tello describes the benefits of the plan that Doña Inés invents to prevent her father from marrying her to Don Rodrigo; that is, by pretending to enter the convent, Inés will buy time for herself. In addition, explains Tello:

También es linda ocasión
para que yo vaya y venga
con libertad a esta casa.

[It also gives me a nice chance / to go in and out / of this house at will.]

. . .

Pues ha de leer latín,
¿no será fácil que pueda
ser yo quien venga a enseñarla?

[Since she has to read Latin / couldn't it be arranged / that I be the one to come and teach her?]

. . .

Y aún pienso que podrá Fabia
servirte en forma de dueña,
siendo la santa mujer
que con su falsa apariencia
venga a enseñarla.

[And also, I think Fabia / could serve you as a maid, / in the guise of / a saintly woman / who will teach her.]

(2.1279–81, 1283–85, 1289–93)

Lope has created a frame around this theatrical game; his characters, self-consciously aware that they have assumed new roles in an interior play, direct their performances toward deceiving their new audience, Inés's father. Language becomes the medium for effecting this deception. The use of Latin, puns, and double entendres as an essential part of this interior play is a technique called suspension, one in which playing the game becomes everything. Suspension virtually blocks off all other forms of dramatic or semantic information in the pursuit of playing the game (Elam 18–19). Of course, as soon as we discover and uncover the game, as soon as we realize how it has been framed, we also realize how it can function to create dramatic irony or to communicate other information to an audience.

To cite a specific example of how suspension works, Fabia, disguised as a holy woman, sets up a parallel between God (or, more specifically, Christ), whom Inés will marry if she becomes a nun, and Inés's suitor, Don Alonso. Fabia plays with the power of words to obfuscate as well as to reveal meaning, telling Inés and her father that the *Señor* whom Inés will marry "es muy noble caballero" [is a very noble gentleman/knight] (2.1425); she further adds that Inés

no ha de casarse en Medina:
monasterio tiene Olmedo;
Domine, si tanto puedo,
ad iuvandum me festina.

[shouldn't get married in Medina: / Olmedo has a monastery; / O Lord, if it is in my power to ask, / make haste to help me.]

(2.1458–61)

Everyone but Inés's father understands Fabia to mean that Inés will marry Alonso, not Christ; her home will be Alonso's house in

Olmedo, not the convent. This game is also made self-conscious through connotation, since the Latin quotation, from *Psalms*, reads, "Make haste to help me, O Lord," which underscores this humorous supplication on the part of Fabia. The word-plays and double entendres above are heightened by the use of Latin in a verbal game that stresses code-switching, utilized here for comic effect. Fabia's use of the language of the church to pray for divine help in bringing about deception is an exaggerated and conspicuous language game, which stands out from other games in the play because of its burlesque nature. In other words, the game, which involves the obtrusive use of two languages, not-so-veiled allusions, and wordplay, becomes the object of the scene itself. It serves therefore to reveal irony, calling attention to the difference between the father's expectations and reality by stressing game playing itself, and by showing that Inés's father is the pawn in a much larger game—one whose rules he does not know.

The world-creating game "brings into play . . . the represented fictional context of the dramatic world" (Elam 13). World-creating games consequently focus upon expository and referential uses of language. Lope uses a great number of language games of this type in *El caballero de Olmedo*. The reason is apparent: the elements of the *comedia de capa y espada* [cloak and sword play] and the *comedia de enredo* [play with a tangled plot] seen in the first two acts of the play reveal the need for the characters to try continually to identify one another—in person and in motive—as the dramatic action becomes increasingly complicated. The female characters are particularly adroit at creating and obfuscating references to themselves and to other characters. Fabia, for example, makes direct reference to herself as a seller of cosmetics and unguents for the face, a laundress, a go-between in affairs of the heart, and a holy woman, and she alludes to herself as a witch. Doña Inés and her sister willingly support Fabia in her impersonations and instigate others, including Tello's disguise as a Latin teacher.

All of these complications are accompanied by linguistic markers that are designed to call attention to deictics and other referential or expository information. The two letters in the play—Don Alonso's love letter to Doña Inés and her response—underline this idea in which the two lovers play games with questions of identity. Fabia's first trip to Inés's house includes the delivery of Alonso's love letter to Inés, and she returns with one from Inés to Alonso. In both cases, the writers try not to reveal too much while they simultaneously ask for more information, attempting to ascertain the other's identity without giving their own away. Don Alonso's letter begins with the words:

> Yo vi la más hermosa labradora,
> en la feria de Medina,
>
> [I saw the most beautiful peasant girl / in the Fair of Medina,]
> (1.503–5)

while Inés's letter starts:

> Cuidadosa de saber si sois quien presumo, y deseando que lo seáis, os suplico que vais esta noche a la reja del jardín desta casa.
>
> [Anxious to know if you are the one I think you are, and hoping that you are that one, I implore you to go tonight to the grilled window by the garden of this house.]

A self-conscious format frames these flirtatious exchanges—that of written letters embedded or boxed within the main text and within the main performance. Elam discusses the use of embedded texts by noting that "Most of the comedies include at least one internal 'textual' event—the reading of a poem, say, or of a letter—placed within the main performance . . ." (25).[5] The letters are not only texts of one generic type embedded within another, but are further commented upon by the other characters as objects, a fact that emphasizes their self-reflexive nature even more.

Other examples of world-creating games appear in the last act of the play, with reference to specific moments in time and space. Don Alonso's physical movement between Olmedo and Medina, between his parents' home and Inés's, has been noted in several critical studies of the play.[6] The appearances of the *sombra* [shadow] and the *labrador* [peasant] further mark the road to Olmedo as the site of the potential tragedy, and the dark night provides the ambushers with the opportunity to kill Don Alonso. In this last act, references to time and place are heightened through repetition, as Lope builds layers of deictic motifs that ultimately presage the protagonist's death.

A third category of language games is that of semantic games, those concerned with producing meaning, in the sense that they deal with the "linguistic sign, its relationship with the extra-linguistic world and the sense relationships *between* signs" (Elam 14). In *El caballero de Olmedo,* there is one semantic game that is overtly framed by connotation through embedded references to a pre-existing literary text: *La Celestina.* In the following quotation, Don Alonso's discourse parallels Calisto's famous "Melibeo soy" [I am Melibean] speech:

Inés me quiere; yo adoro
a Inés, yo vivo en Inés.
Todo lo que Inés no es
desprecio, aborrezco, ignoro.
Inés es mi bien; yo soy
esclavo de Inés.

[Inés loves me; I adore / Inés, I live in Inés. / All that Inés is not / I despise, hate, ignore. / Inés is my darling; I am / the slave of Inés.]
(2.988–93)

This semantic game, which has linked the linguistic sign "Inés" to Don Alonso's self-definition, is further framed by a reference even more explicit. Tello asks Doña Inés's servant:

¿Está en casa Melibea?
Que viene Calisto aquí,

[Is Melibea at home? / For Calisto is coming over.]

to which the servant replies:

Aguarda un poco, Sempronio.

[Wait a little bit, Sempronio.]
(2.1003–5)

Lope has embedded these literary allusions within the fabric of the dramatic world of *El caballero de Olmedo.* He frames the game by self-consciously tracing the links between the linguistic sign and its relationship with the extratextual reality of the linguistic signs of an antecedent text. The stylistic and textual origins of this scene illustrate how connotation works: it can bring recollections of the *Celestina* to the surface while simultaneously demythologizing them, using instantly recognizable motifs in contexts that only further reinforce the distance between these motifs and the original text.

Semantic games and their ties to connotation are an important element of *El caballero de Olmedo.* Equally important are the kinds of language games that emphasize *how* characters use language within the world defined onstage. Elam observes that

> within the fictional world itself the dramatic *personae* are taken to be directly engaged in talk. This, of course, is the chief institutional difference between drama and narrative: the dramatic fiction is not so much narrated as *conversed* . . . much of the dramatic and comic energy of the play is invested in the maintenance of the fictional conversational exchange. (15)

Pragmatic games are closely related to these "conversational and interactional functions" and, as such, have to do with turn-taking, hogging the floor, speaking sincerely or insincerely, and responding appropriately or inappropriately (15). In *El caballero de Olmedo,* two pragmatic games stand out. The first has to do with Doña Inés's failures to inform her father that she prefers to marry Don Alonso and not Don Rodrigo. Her insistence on speaking insincerely to her own father and on responding inappropriately (or not at all) to his suggestions about her future lead to the tragic events of the end of the play. Lope ironically points out that this deception was completely unnecessary. When Inés's sister finally blurts out the truth, their father responds that had he known about Inés's desires, he would not have opposed her marriage to Don Alonso.

The other side of this type of language game is Don Alonso's refusal to heed the numerous warnings offered by the *sombra* [shadow] and *labrador* [peasant]. If Doña Inés has witheld information that could help her cause, Don Alonso has received valuable information but refuses to heed it. His dying words echo his recognition that he reacted inappropriately to prior warnings:

> ¡Qué poco crédito di
> a los avisos del cielo!
> Valor propio me ha engañado,
> y muerto envidias y celos.

> [How little credit I gave / to Heaven's forewarning! / My own courage has deceived me, / envy and jealousy have slain me.]
>
> (3.2465–68)

These two pragmatic games underscore the irony of *El caballero de Olmedo* as they focus on the two central acts of giving and heeding conversational cues.

The final type of language game that Elam explores is the

figural game. Elam contends that rhetorical figures may be seen as very active "*doings* with words," functioning together or separately as an underlying series of textual strategies that move the dramatic action forward (16). The analysis above has already alluded to the code-switching of the scenes in which Tello poses as a Latin teacher and to the comic and structural functions of the metaphoric reference to extracting a tooth: "sacar una dama de su casa" [abducting a lady from her house]. Critics such as William McCrary, Alison Turner, and Willard King have examined similar rhetorical figures in their studies of the imagery and symbolism of the goldfinch and the hawk, the Cruz de Mayo, and the phoenix. In each case, these figures define the structural foundation upon which the dramatic action is based. I would further add that the figural games just described are framed by self-conscious repetition and embedded allusions to other texts, which only further emphasizes their metatheatrical nature.

One final example can illustrate the tightness of Lope's style, as well as the ways in which the dramatist strategically uses figural games within *El Caballero de Olmedo*. In act 1, Alonso explains his love sickness to Fabia, asking for her help in securing Inés's favors. In typically lyrical fashion, Alonso describes Inés's teeth as pearls and her cheeks as coral. He then goes on to describe a communicative exchange effected through the eyes:

> Yo, haciendo lengua los ojos,
> solamente le ofrecía
> a cada cabello un alma,
> a cada paso una vida.
> Mirándome sin hablarme,
> parece que me decía:
> "No os vais, don Alonso, a Olmedo,
> quedaos agora en Medina."

[I, making my eyes my own tongue / could only offer her one soul for each strand of hair / one life for each of her footsteps. / As she looked at me without words, it seems to me that she said: / "Don't go to Olmedo, don Alonso, / stay in Medina this time."]

(1.127–34)

By using such figures as synecdoche, anaphora, and metaphor in a stanza dealing with the act of communication Lope heightens their effect. That effect, however, is further intensified in this particular example, because the passage itself blatantly stresses nonverbal communication. As a result, the excerpt underscores the irony of what Doña Inés is supposedly telling Don Alonso: that he not go to Olmedo, but that he should stay in Medina. Even this apparently innocent remark in a very early scene forecasts the realities of act 3: Don Alonso *should* stay in Medina and not go to Olmedo.[7]

The love imagery, metaphors, and other figures in this scene present the protagonist's fate at the end of the play, a fact that is further emphasized a few verses later, when Don Alonso follows Inés and her sister into church:

> En una capilla entraron;
> yo, que siguiéndolas iba,
> entré imaginando bodas:
> ¡tanto quien ama imagina!
> Vime sentenciado a muerte,
> porque el amor me decía:
> "Mañana mueres, pues hoy
> te meten en la capilla."

> [They entered a chapel; / I followed them / and entered too, imagining a wedding: / a lover imagines so much! / I saw myself sentenced to death, / because love was saying to me: / "Tomorrow you will die, for today / they have put you in the chapel."]
>
> (1.151–58)

The connections between love and death are obvious here, and examples such as these abound in *El caballero de Olmedo,* forming part of a carefully constructed system of metaphorical references and images that structures the drama. Lope has framed the figural games of Alonso's love lament as part of an overall theatrical strategy that links the first two acts with the third and illustrates clearly how language games can be activated in his play.

It should be noted that the richness of the final scenes of *El caballero de Olmedo* is due, in great measure, to the culmination or reunion of images—and language games—that have built, one upon the other, throughout the play. In that sense, the arrival of the shadow, the *sombra,* marks a decisive point in the dramatic action, since that moment allows Don Alonso to meet his fate:

> *Don Alonso.* ¿Qué es esto? ¿Quién va? De oírme
> no hace caso. ¿Quién es? Hable.
> ¡Que un hombre me atemorice,
> no habiendo temido a tantos!

¿Es don Rodrigo? ¿No dice
quién es?
Sombra. Don Alonso.
Don Alonso. ¿Cómo?
Sombra. Don Alonso.
Don Alonso. No es posible.
Mas otro será, que yo
soy don Alonso Manrique. . . .

[*D. Alonso.* What is this? Who is there? He doesn't listen / to me. Who is it? Speak. / How can one man scare me, / after not having feared so many! / Is it Don Rodrigo? Won't you say / who you are? / *Shadow.* Don Alonso. / *D. Alonso.* What? / *Shadow.* Don Alonso. / *D. Alonso.* It's not possible. It must be someone else, because I am Don Alonso Manrique. . . .]

. . .
Mi sombra debió de ser. . . .
Mas no, que en forma visible
dijo que era don Alonso.
Todas son cosas que finge
la fuerza de la tristeza,
la imaginación de un triste.

[It must have been my own shadow. . . / But it can't be: in a visible form it said / that it was Don Alonso. / All this is something / created by my own sadness, / a sad man's imagination.]

(3.2257–65, 2270–75)

Don Alonso continues his quest for possible explanations for the appearance of the *sombra,* proposing "embustes de Fabia" [Fabia's lies] and "que don Rodrigo me envidie" [Don Rodrigo's envy] as other reasons for the arrival of this masked figure who is dressed in black. Don Alonso concludes, however, that none of these explanations is correct, and he continues on his way, only to be met and killed by Don Rodigro and his band of men.

This scene is framed in a wholly self-conscious manner. In one sense, it represents the culmination of the images presaging the protagonist's death, as our discussion of figural games suggested. The masked, shadowy figure incarnates images of death, and his appearance onstage is part of a physically symbolic and linguistically balanced scene. Don Alonso begins and ends this section. In the first part, he asks four questions and comments upon them himself, almost as if the questions were purely rhetorical.

Furthermore, the fact that he poses these questions aloud helps to highlight Don Alonso's fears; with no other interlocutors around, his speaking out loud represents a kind of "whistling in the dark."

The middle section of this fragment could be diagrammed as a perfect parallel construction, A / B / A, as the *sombra* reveals himself:

Sombra. Don Alonso.
Don Alonso. ¿Cómo?
Sombra. Don Alonso.

[*Shadow.* Don Alonso. / *D. Alonso.* What? / *Shadow.* Don Alonso.]
(3.2262–63)

This middle section is followed by Don Alonso's attempt to explain in rational terms what he has seen and heard and by his rejection of the *sombra* as an omen presaging his death. Lope has given us a scene that centers on questions and answers, on a search for information, and on a concomitant denial of it. The *sombra*'s repetition of the two words, "Don Alonso," forces us to focus our attention on the question of identity and its relationship to the protagonist's death.

As a result, this scene also suggests a language game that unites the theatrical (framed as metatheatrical) and world-creating games. It is world-creating in that Don Alonso's questions about the identity of the *sombra* represent an attempt to deal in a concrete manner with the ways that language relates to reference and to exposition. This world-creating game is framed, however, by Don Alonso's recognition that he is talking to himself, to his own refracted image. His attempt to identify the shadow has led the character to see the part of himself that is—and, simultaneously, is not—a part of the reality of his world. The scene between Don Alonso and the *sombra* therefore explores the conflict between appearance and reality, while it frames the language game in which Don Alonso seeks to establish the *sombra*'s identity. As such, it also puts a frame around itself in a metatheatrical sense. As one character confronts his other, doubled self, his future is revealed: Don Alonso has met his destiny, one that is marked by shadows, the ominous color black, and death. Character meets character in an unearthly parody of more ordinary theatrical interaction; their dialogue therefore reveals itself as highly self-conscious, since we realize that these two men are really two aspects of the same dramatic figure.

This analysis has used Elam's and Wittgenstein's notions of the language game as a guide for exploring what happens in *El caballero de Olmedo,* but it is, by necessity, merely an introduction to the possibilities that Wittgenstein offers to *comedia* scholars. Elam's study summarizes Shakespeare's universe of discourse as a typically baroque construct in that it displays formal self-reflection, self-mirroring metatexts, and metacommentaries, emphasizing the idea that Shakespeare's game-frame dialectic presents "language placed (structurally, thematically, theatrically) *en abyme*" (23). It is fitting to close with the reminder that Elam's comments regarding Shakespeare's framed games are strikingly relevant to Lope and to *El caballero de Olmedo.* The language game, self-consciously framed throughout *El caballero de Olmedo,* can help us better understand the union of words and actions in the play. In that sense, theory and practice can come together as we explore the ways that twentieth-century interpretive tools can help to unlock the mysteries of seventeenth-century texts.

5

La dama duende and the Shifting Characterization of Calderón's Diabolical Angel

> What may most distinguish the new literary movement called feminist criticism is precisely its effort to bring to consciousness . . . ancient, half-conscious questions about textuality and sexuality.
>
> —Sandra Gilbert

The kinds of approaches to language that we have examined up to this point have dealt with issues of power and authority, naming and reference, membership in linguistic communities, and rule-breaking within those communities of speakers, specifically from the perspective of viewing speech as action. In a very real sense, the following analysis incorporates all of these ideas, but also adds another dimension: it is grounded in the relationship between language and gender. Our examination of these issues focuses upon the union of feminist and linguistic approaches to literature, specifically as they relate to a Calderonian comedy, *La dama duende* [*The Spirit Lady*]. The articulation of feminist issues in the theater of Calderón is very much open to textual explication due to the fact that feminist literary theory and criticism have established themselves as determinant ideological and methodological forces only in the past fifteen years. Therefore, critics interested in the ways that a male writer presented his female characters will find that we can learn more about the ways those characters were portrayed.

This portrayal of women relates to the fact that in seventeenth-century Spanish drama, in an era in which the characterization of women tended to follow rather conventionalized modes of expression, female characters were presented with a generally limited range of types, including the standard, beautiful *dama* [lady], the *mujer esquiva* [disdainful woman], the religious woman, the *mujer vestida de hombre* [woman dressed as a man] , and the married woman/victim of the wife-murder plays. Calderón, a product of seventeenth-century attitudes concerning women, was undoubtedly influenced by the mores of his age. Nonetheless, recent discussions have led to new readings of Golden Age drama; feminism has entered the critical arena of *comedia* studies. This chapter addresses Calderón's constantly-shifting characterization of one of his most famous female characters, Doña Angela from *La dama duende*. As we will see, Calderón's depiction of this woman reveals a signifying process that both upholds and subverts the tradition of which he is a part.

The first issue raised here is how to integrate a feminist reading into plays written by dramatists who were male and who wrote in a time in which male-female relationships would have to be judged as extremely unliberated by today's standards. A socio-feminist approach, which examines images of women in literature, would emphasize what Toril Moi has called "the way in which writers constantly *select* the elements they wish to use in their texts" (*Sexual/Textual Politics* 45). Yet, in addition, Moi observes that "no criticism is 'value-free'" (43): we always make our own critical assessments of an author's decisions based on the tradition from which we come, one that is still inherently patriarchal. Elaine Showalter has been a leading proponent of the notions that women approach texts differently than men and that male writers frequently operate from within the bounds of a patriarchal system. Showalter observes that "one of the problems of the feminist critique is that it is male-oriented. If we study stereotypes of women, the sexism of male critics, and the limited roles women play in literary history, we are not learning what women have felt and experienced, but only what men have thought women should be" ("Towards a Feminist Poetics" 130). In that context, I would like to suggest that we need to explore how discussions of women in the *comedia* can move beyond mere attacks on the sexism of androtexts in order to lead us to new levels of interpretation. I am positing a revision of the critical canon, but from within a kind of feminist perspective that allows new thought on how Calderón depicts his women to join with, rather than to supplant completely, traditional critical approaches to his plays.

With regard to *La dama duende,* those traditional views often reveal a great deal about what happens when male critics confront texts written by men about women. Robert ter Horst's work with *La dama duende* is a useful example, in which he states that "in *La dama duende,* the dominant masculine order intrudes upon a feminine chaos and masters it . . ." ("The Ruling Temper" 72). He further observes that the central issue of *La dama duende* is not, as Edwin Honig had suggested, "a woman's rebellion against the (honor) code's autocratic male principles" (*Calderón and the Seizures of Honor* 110). Rather, ter Horst contends that the main character of the play is Don Manuel, "whose masculine hierarchy is superior in the art of life and civilization to Angela's chaos" (72). This view of Don Manuel as a *paterfamilias,* as a tamer of "his splendid shrew" (72), clearly proffers a phallocentric reading of the play. I do not, however, mean to suggest a wholly negative response to that point of view. Instead, I see ter Horst's article as exemplary of the patriarchal critical tradition in which we all have been trained, one that focuses, as in this case, on androcentric issues of superiority and dominance and on the opposition of order to chaos.[1] I would nonetheless suggest a counter reading, one that illuminates the precarious position that defines the essence of the title character. To do so, I will examine Calderón's signifying practices in the classification and representation of his diabolical angel.

As a typical *comedia de capa y espada* [cloak and sword play], *La dama duende* deals with disguise, plot complications, and problems of determining identity. The use of disguise is central to any examination of the role of women in the *comedia* and in this play, since it implies that women often must resort to using disguises and masks when they can't get what they want in more socially acceptable ways. In *La dama duende,* these disguises are both physical and linguistic. In semiotic terms, we could describe Doña Angela as the referent; she is an object, the mystery woman who is pursued early in the play by her brother, Don Luis, and, later, by Don Manuel. The signs pointing toward that referent consist of signifieds (that is, the men's concepts or images of the woman) and signifiers (all of the words representing her). As we shall see, both the signifieds and the signifiers function on different levels for the male characters of the play and for Angela herself. Further, since signs cannot express a one-to-one correspondence with the referent but can only signal or point toward it, we know that countless numbers of signs endlessly defer to the future the possibility of determining absolute truth in identity; they can never reveal it completely.[2]

In this play, the signifieds and signifiers, the concepts and language describing the woman, frequently emerge as contradictions that impede the exact revelation of the referent: Calderón presents his unknown woman as both devil and angel. The signs that Calderón uses to describe Angela, however, are constantly shifting, for she is neither an angel nor a devil, and is, at the same time, both—although, even more importantly, by the end of the play, the principal sign used to characterize her is "woman." In that sense, we might suggest that the mystery woman is both disguised and illuminated throughout the play as the signs describing her converge and separate simultaneously.

Frederick de Armas explains this curious combination of elements (*ángel, demonio y mujer* [angel, demon, and woman]) as characteristic of what he describes as the "Invisible Mistress" plot: "most works dealing with this theme present us with a woman of great (angelical) beauty, whose *burlas* [tricks] are so elaborate that supernatural powers are often attributed to her—be it as a witch, an enchantress, or a *duende* [spirit]" (*The Invisible Mistress* 130). Susan Fischer, on the other hand, surveys not the "Invisible Mistress," but the "Invisible Partner" in *La dama duende.* She views Angela and Manuel as Jungian analogues of each other in which the male, Manuel, finds his own inner female side in the anima, Angela, who leads him through a journey of self-discovery (231–33). Both of these readings suggest a bipartite division (man/woman, angel/devil, *dama/duende,* anima/animus) that ultimately foregrounds a complex baroque vision of the characterization in *La dama duende.*[3] By focusing on the interplay of these opposing elements—and their synthesis in the concept *woman*—we may better appreciate how a male writer such as Calderón fashioned a character like Doña Angela, who is independently strong and stereotypically weak, successful and unsuccessful in achieving her goals, beneficent and maleficent.

There are apparently two "Angelas" in this play: the character who is the widowed sister of Don Juan and Don Luis and the woman who appears as the disguised object of Don Manuel's desire, the *dama duende* seen by Don Manuel and his servant. We know, of course, that they are one and the same woman. Yet, even these two apparently different women can be subdivided into two opposing aspects: angel and devil. The first Doña Angela, the widowed sister, has a scheming side; she possesses a number of qualities that link her to the licentiousness and machinations associated with the devil, at least within the scope of seventeenth-century culture and religion. First, Angela defines herself when she describes flirtatious women, saying that such a coquette is "una mala mujer . . . una mujer tramoyera" [an evil woman . . . a scheming woman; literally, "tramoya" means stage machinery] (1.515, 517). Angela *is* witty and deceitful; Calderón's choice of the word "tramoyera" indicates that Doña Angela well understands the stagecraft needed to pull off the theatrical illusions of her own dramas with the male characters—dramas that, from a theatrical point of view, self-consciously involve going in and out of the secret doorway that is hidden behind the cupboard in Don Manuel's bedroom and the playing of roles within her "normal" role.[4] Calderón details the reasons for that characterization when a maid explains why widows have such a bad reputation:

> este estado
> es el más ocasionado
> a delitos amorosos;
> a más en la Corte hoy,
> donde se han dado en usar
> unas viuditas de azahar.

[this state / is the most given / to amorous offenses; / even more so at Court today, / where certain little perfumed widows / have surrendered themselves for use.]

(1.405–11)

Operating from a seventeenth-century male-dominant perspective, then, Calderón describes widows at court as synonymous with loose, scheming women.[5]

Furthermore, the type of character described above is part of a cultural and literary tradition that associates women with the devil in terms of cunning and manipulation and as a symbolic recreation of Eve, whose curiosity in the Garden of Eden leads her to taste the fruit of the Tree of Knowledge.[6] Melveena McKendrick notes that the identification of women with the devil was still very much a part of Spanish tradition as recently as the appearance of Luis de León's *La perfecta casada* [The Perfect Wife], written less than fifty years prior to *La dama duende* (*Woman and Society* 10–11).

Calderón's Angela fulfills this definition: she steals out of her house in disguise in order to flirt with the men of the court. Only when her brother pursues her does she begin to recognize the dangerous implications of her game. Angela's curiosity about Don Manuel leads her to manipulate him by assuming the role of the *dama duende,* although those actions put her in even more danger. A young widow whose honor has been fiercely guarded by her two brothers, Angela acquires a new and unsavory reputation when, at the end of the play, her brothers describe her as a *traidora* [traitor] and *fiera* [wild animal or vixen]. These characterizations could lead to terrible consequences for the young woman. Her life is literally at stake, since even the implication of her sexual misconduct could damage reputations, destroy honor, and lead her brothers to take Angela's life. Both through her own actions and discourse and the comments of others, Angela is associated with a number of negative qualities that link her metonymically to Eve and the forbidden apple of the Garden of Eden.

Still, Angela is also a martyr, buried alive (as she says) "entre dos paredes" [between two walls] (1.380). Her two overprotective brothers keep her locked up at home dressed in mourning clothes, when, as a young, noble, and beautiful woman, she yearns for the freedom and excitement offered by the men outside the walls of her "prison":

> sin libertad he vivido,
> porque me enviudé de un marido,
> con dos hermanos casada.

> [I have lived without freedom, / since although I've been widowed, / I'm married to two brothers.]
>
> (1.390–92)

Angela has also suffered as the result of debts incurred by her late husband; her economic martyrdom further underscores the sympathetic aspects of her character. Finally, and most obviously, the protagonist's very name suggests angelic associations. The signifier that Calderón selected to identify Doña Angela could certainly not have been chosen at random: the beautiful angel is given a name designed to suggest her essence. In fact, when Don Manuel first sees his *dama duende,* he exclaims, "¡Un asombro de belleza, / un ángel hermoso es!" [An astonishing beauty, / she's a beautiful angel!] (2.2059–60). We see, then, that the language used to fix Doña Angela's identity covers the entire spectrum of possible signifiers: positive and negative, sympathetic and accusatory, angelic and diabolical.[7]

The other "Angela," the mysterious woman who keeps appearing to Don Manuel and his servant Cosme, is, of course, the *dama duende,* who also combines the opposing elements of angel and devil. Cosme, the superstitious *gracioso,* perceives her devilish qualities from the very beginning, describing her as a *demonio,* a *duende,* or, at the very least, a *mujer-diablo:*

> Que es mujer-diablo;
> pues que novedad no es,
> pues la mujer es demonio
> todo el año, que una vez,

por desquitarse de tantas,
sea el demonio mujer.

[She's a devil-woman; / of course, that's nothing new; / since women are devils / all year long, for once / let the devil turn into a woman / just to even the score.]

(2.2237–42)

The *gracioso* consistently upholds the traditional link between women and the devil. In the third act of the play, Cosme is led into an "enchanted" room, and he tells the story of Lucifer dressing as a woman in order to seduce a shepherd, concluding:

aún horrible no es
en traje en hembra,
un demonio.

[even a demon / isn't so horrible / when he's dressed in women's clothes.]

(3.2661–62)

This story, along with Cosme's description of the *dama duende* as a succuba, lends a note of sexual rebellion to the description of Doña Angela, pushing her even further beyond the limits of socially acceptable behavior. The *dama duende* embodies associations with the heavens and with hell, reinforcing the tension between angels and demons, and both Cosme and Don Manuel are literally and metaphorically left in the dark as to her identity.[8]

* * *

In their explorations of the identity of the literary female, Sandra Gilbert and Susan Gubar describe the image of woman as angel and as monster in an analysis that offers many points of contact with this study of Calderón and *La dama duende.* These two critics posit that "the ideal woman that male writers dream of generating is always an angel"; they trace the image from the Middle Ages and the Virgin Mary through Dante, Milton, and Goethe to the nineteenth century's "angel in the house" of Victorian literature.[9] The ideal of the eternal feminine was, for these male writers, represented by pure, passive, and powerless female types, "for in the metaphysical emptiness their 'purity' signifies, they are, of course, *self-less,* with all the moral and psychological implications that word suggests" (*The Madwoman in the Attic* 21). For the Victorian woman—and, I would maintain, for the heroine of Golden Age texts—the surrender of self was considered "the beautiful angel woman's key act" (25). Yet, numerous literary texts associate the submissive angel with ghosts and sprites; she is also capable of scheming and manipulation by refusing to stay in her ordained place. She displays a negative side that Gilbert and Gubar label monstrous—and that Calderón would have described as devilish or demonic—which functions in opposition to her angelic side.

Certainly, these views on the angel and demon or monster that simultaneously exist in many of the female characters that male writers have penned are directly applicable to our reading of *La dama duende*. Doña Angela, rebelling against the loss of self demanded by masculine perceptions of the eternal feminine, is both the angel and monster in her house. Even more significantly, although her assertiveness and manipulation, revealed in her role as the phantom lady, challenge the notion of the ideal woman, Calderón nonetheless leaves us with a woman who will again typify patriarchal definitions of the feminine at the conclusion of the play. As we will soon discuss, the challenge to patriarchal authority that the phantom lady incarnates is subsumed at the end of act 3 by the vision of Angela as adoring lover, as wife, and as the "angel in the house."

Angela herself complicates the already tangled plot, setting up barriers to confuse the male characters in the play. This Calderonian woman knows the most successful approaches for appealing to male vanity, seeking compassion based on her position as a weak and unhappy woman as, for example, when she asks Manuel for help:

> Si, como lo muestra
> el traje, sois caballero
> de obligaciones y prendas,
> amparad a una mujer.

[If, as your clothing suggests, / you are a gentleman / of honor and means, / defend a woman.]

(1.101–4)

At other times, she presents herself as a foolish, empty-headed member of her gender:

> Yo fui necia en empeñarle así;
> mas una mujer turbada
> ¿qué mira o qué considera?

> [I was silly to urge him on so; / but a frightened woman, / what does she see or consider?]
>
> (1.437–40)

Yet, Calderón paints an even more detailed portrait of his protagonist. Doña Angela's actions are particularly revealing when she combines the conflictive elements of her character with the tricks that she plays on Don Manuel. Angela secretly leaves him gifts that include sweets and clothing, and she invites him to a banquet in which she creates the impression that she is a wealthy member of royalty. In each case, Doña Angela acts as the traditional "angel in the house," nurturing her man by giving him food and clean clothes. Nonetheless, each example of Angela's "angelic" role-playing is also tied to deception and manipulation.[10]

Indeed, Angela's characterization is so complex that sometimes even she can describe herself only in terms of absence. When Manuel uses conventionalized love vocabulary to describe her as "aurora, sol y alba" [dawn, sun, and daybreak], Angela replies:

> lo que soy ignoro;
> que sólo sé que no soy
> alba, aurora o sol.

> [I don't know what I am; / I only know that I'm not / the dawn, daybreak, or sun.]
>
> (3.2350–51)

Angela, who has been characterized throughout the play by a multitude of signifiers, ironically finds herself at a loss for words, particularly when those words operate within a semiotic system based on instant identification between the sign and its referent—here, between nature (the dawn and the sun) and the beautiful woman who serves as the subject of poetic inspiration.

Angela is a character marked by the opposition of presence and absence. Her mysterious appearances and disappearances through the hidden door covered by the *alacena* [cupboard] are emblematic of her role as both the present and absent object of Don Manuel's desire. This conflict is further repeated in the "flickers of incest" motif noted by Honig, which involves Don Luis's pursuit of his own disguised sister (117). Presence and absence surface in both situations when Angela, the widow lacking a male protector, begs Manuel to assume the roles of suitor and savior. The absence of a husband must be negated through substitutes who fulfill patriarchal definitions and serve as male providers and protectors. Finally, the opposition of presence and absence suggests yet another level of interpretation in the play, that of discourse, since signs always contain within themselves traces of their radical opposites. The presence of "angel" always signals the absence of "devil"; consequently, any definition of Doña Angela as ingenious or manipulative allows for that which is not ingenious or manipulative—in other words, that which is angelic in nature. Calderón both negates and synthesizes these metaphoric oppositions in Angela's "real" role—that of woman.

In a key confrontation scene at the end of act 2, Calderón has his characters bring together the central aspects of the phantom lady. Manuel surprises Angela in his room:

Angel, demonio, o mujer,
a fe que no has de librarte
de mis manos esta vez.

[Angel, demon, or woman, / I swear you'll not slip / through my hands this time.]

(2.2080–82)

Angela tries to defer revealing her true identity until the following day, but Manuel replies:

Mujer, quien quiera que seas,
que no tengo de creer
que eras otra cosa nunca,
¡vive Dios, que he de saber
quién eres, cómo has entrado
aquí, con qué fin, y a qué!
Sin esperar a mañana
esta dicha gozaré;
si demonio, por demonio,
y si mujer, por mujer;

[Woman, whoever you may be, / and I don't believe that you're anything else, / By God, I will find out / who you are, how you entered / here, for what end, and what you plan to do! / Without waiting until tomorrow / I intend to enjoy this delight, / if you're a devil, as a devil, / if you're a woman, as a woman.]

(2.2123–32)

When Manuel threatens to kill her, Angela confesses that she is only "una infelice mujer" [an unhappy woman] (2.2152), but after she manages to slip away from him again, Manuel is left puzzled:

Como sombra se mostró;
fantástica su luz fue
pero como cosa humana,
se dejó tocar y ver;
como mortal se temió,
receló como mujer,
como ilusión se deshizo,
como fantasma se fue.
Si doy la rienda al discurso,
no sé, ¡vive Dios! no sé
ni qué tengo de dudar,
ni qué tengo de creer.

[She appeared like a shadow; / gleaming fantastically / but as something human, / she let herself be touched and seen; / she was afraid as a mortal would be, / as an illusion she vanished, / as a ghost she left. / If I give rein to this idea, / I don't know—dear God, I don't know / what I should doubt, / and what I believe.]

(2.2225–36)

We find that throughout much of the play Don Manuel is unable to verify the identity of his phantom lady. Calderón's demonic angel remains an enigma. Even in act 3, she continues to cloud herself in mystery: "ni soy lo que parezco, / ni parezco lo que soy" [I'm not what I seem to be, / and I don't seem to be what I am] (3.2375–76).

The *dama duende* finally identifies herself at the end of act 3 by uttering a simple statement that removes her from the realm of the supernatural and confirms her essence, that which both is and is not conveyed by the concept of angel or devil: "una mujer soy y fui" [I was and am a woman] (3.2355). When she finally explains that she is the sister of Don Juan and Don Luis, Angela clarifies the identity question that has been plaguing Don Manuel. This, of course, only leads to further confusion in Doña Angela's complex characterization, since the flesh-and-blood sister also incarnates both angelic and devilish qualities. All of the linguistic signifiers used to characterize her (*fiera, torbellino, duende, mujer, ángel, diablo* [wild beast, whirlwind, spirit, woman, angel, devil]) join with the varying concepts that the male characters have of this woman, creating signs that can never completely and concretely define the referent, precisely because they indicate that she is—and is not—a composite of essences.

The idea that Angela is an amalgam of opposing concepts or images, as well as concomitantly opposing signifiers, is central to Calderón's treatment of his female character. For each of the male characters, Doña Angela is many things, including a beautiful woman, a widowed sister needing protection, a phantom lady, a veiled woman running from a man, the object of amorous desire, a giver of gifts, and the noble hostess of a fantastic banquet. These images of the woman are part of a constantly shifting mosaic and are underscored by a variety of signifiers that the male characters use in their attempts to attach a definition to her. The men in Doña Angela's life describe her in terms of malevolence and benevolence, as a weak woman and as an independent spirit, as the devil's helpmate and as an angelic essence. The varied linguistic markers that they use point, on a negative level, to a certain degree of ambiguity in Angela's characterization, and on a positive level, to a richly evolving character, incarnating not a stereotypical view of the seventeenth-century Spanish woman, but rather the image of a complex, well-rounded dramatic character who can be understood by modern audiences.

In that sense we can appreciate the enigmatic quality of the ultimate definition of Doña Angela, one that she gives to herself: "soy / mucho más de lo que ves" [I'm / much more than what you see] (2.2167–68). It is here, finally, that Calderón's protagonist moves beyond sexual stereotyping and expresses the complexity of her character. Angela is not merely angelic because of her beauty, or devilish because of her ingenuity and manipulative actions. Although such stereotyping serves the creation of the kinds of baroque oppositions for which Calderón is famous, we should note that Angela is both (and neither) angel and devil—and that she truly *is* much more than she appears to be. This leads us to the ending of the play and to its implications with regard to Calderón's treatment of his female characters.

In many ways, Calderón's protagonist challenges the patriarchal notion that women cannot act as independent spirits and that they cannot play a major role in determining their own destinies. The dramatist foregrounds this concept by having his character act in a theatrically self-conscious manner. We have already discussed the self-conscious nature of Angela's use of the theatrical term, *tramoya* [stage machinery]. In addition, Angela creates a play within the play in which she not only stars as the phantom lady, but she also casts Don Manuel as her lover and takes a firm hand in directing the course of the dramatic action.

This play within the play consists of two main components: the scenes in which Doña Angela leaves notes and gifts for Manuel (prompting his subsequent responses) and the most clearly metadramatic scene, the one in which Angela adopts the role of noble hostess at a banquet to which Manuel is brought. In the scenes of the first type, Angela does not directly confront Manuel, but rather leads him to react in response to requests and presents left by her mysterious alter ego, the *dama duende.* Manuel responds by assuming a new role as well. After reading her letters, he decides to imitate a literary character, becoming the "Cavallero de la Dama Duende" [Knight of the Dama Duende], an avatar of Don Quixote. In this role, Don Manuel adopts a rhetorical style characteristic of the knights of the novels of chivalry; nevertheless, his actions are ultimately guided by the controlling hand of Doña Angela, who has given him a role in the play that she is directing.[11]

Such metatheatrical elements become even more obvious when Angela actually appears in person to Manuel as the hostess at a banquet, although it should be noted that she appears disguised as someone else, with her dialogue rehearsed, with a supporting cast of players, and with a stage clearly set to facilitate the dramatization of her interior play. These self-conscious theatrical gestures highlight the opposition of appearance and reality, as well as the entire notion of role playing, which lies at the heart of Calderón's multifaceted characterization of Doña Angela. In addition, they stress the idea that Angela can challenge societal limitations by acting in an autonomous manner.

Nevertheless, Calderón also shows us that Angela's play carries within itself the potential for tragedy, and that, as we will discuss below, the ending of this comedy reveals a type of social reintegration that undercuts the feminist gains made by his protagonist. Angela, the dramatist, director, and actress, is not quite able to pull off her production without problems. Her independence and ingenuity do lead to her goal of marriage, but marriage will force her back into a more subservient role. Angela's price for theatrical success is a role that will allow her less freedom, independence, and control—at least as far as *comedia* tradition is concerned.

At the end of *La dama duende,* Angela discovers that her life is in real peril and that her brother is engaged in a duel with her lover. She asks Don Manuel to help her, a parallel to her earlier request for masculine protection. In that sense, Doña Angela has come full circle although perhaps, in another sense, she really has not changed at all. The witty woman who has controlled the action of the males of the play now finds herself again in the position of pleading for help, based on her own self-definition as a helpless victim of love and her gender:

> Mi intento fue el quererte,
> mi fin amarte
> . . .
> mi deseo servirte,
> y mi llanto en efeto persuadirte
> que mi daño repares,
> que me valgas, me ayudes y me ampares.

> [My intention was to cherish you, / my goal to love you . . . / my desire to serve you, / and my plea, in effect, to persuade you / to come to my aid, / to defend me, help me, and protect me.]
>
> (3.2997–3004)

We might well speculate that Calderón's overall treatment of Doña Angela is as mutable as are her interior roles of angel and devil, *dama* and *duende*. The Angela of the beginning and end of the play differs markedly from the stronger character who controls the course of the dramatic action throughout most of *La dama duende*. This shifting characterization is highlighted by the nature of the ending of this comedy: the kind of societal reconciliation and reintegration represented in the denouement by the promised marriage of the central characters.

Still, this type of ending is also part of a much larger picture: as K. K. Ruthven observes, "the device of ending stage comedies with a marriage is an economical way of tying up loose narrative ends; but as a device for bringing women legally under the control of men, its popularity as a dramaturgical device is not insignificant in a patriarchal society" (*Feminist Literary Studies* 76). Within the world of the *comedia* weddings acquire special meaning, since we know that the sequel to the marriage of comedy is sometimes the death of the (often) innocent woman in the honor tragedy. We might well wonder about the future of a character like Doña Angela, who has tasted freedom, who has had great success in manipulating men, and who has proven herself clever and resourceful. As Matthew Stroud rightly observes:

> Angela came out all right, but only by undergoing a role-name change from mischievous woman to wife. By the time she makes the change, she has, in effect, lost her former name and identity for the sake of society, a society which does not appreciate her as a clever individual

> intellect (she is almost killed as a result) but only as a sex object or a docile silent wife. ("Social-Comic *Anagnorisis*" 100)

Elaborating on Bruce Wardropper's seminal work on Golden Age comedy, Edward Friedman notes that comedy allows women to "exercise control over the male-dominated world in which they are forced to live," since the "inverted universe of comic drama allows woman the opportunity to assume the role of aggressor. . . . The comic plays . . . reward daring, mettle, ingenuity—in short, active and anti-social behavior—with the desired object, a marriage pledge" ("Girl Gets Boy" 77–78). Yet, these "subversive aspects of drama" described by Friedman are also undermined as "the play progresses toward tragedy, and the playgoers renew their belief in institutions" (78). This is the "Catch-22" that marks Calderón's treatment of his title character. As a woman in a comedy, Doña Angela is allowed to manipulate, even to show herself as superior to the males in the play; still, the seeds of potential tragedy have ironically been sown at the moment of her greatest power and success. Doña Angela, a powerful, affirming figure in most of Calderón's comedy, also carries within her the threat of grave consequences in the future. These oppositions, present-future, comedy-tragedy, vitality-death, only serve to emphasize further the divisions within Doña Angela that mark her characterization in *La dama duende.* Angela, the *dama* and *duende,* the angel, the devil, and the woman, stands out as a character who both subverts and reaffirms the norms of the society of which she is a part, as well as those of her creator.[12] Since she, herself, evolves as the result of a constantly shifting process of signification, Calderón's Doña Angela might well have understood the words of Adrienne Rich:

> A woman in the shape of a monster
> a monster in the shape of a woman
> the skies are full of them.[13]

6

"Violent Hierarchies": The Deconstructive Voice and Writing Undone in *Fuenteovejuna*

Everything we do must be a repetition of the past with a difference.
—William Carlos Williams

In the preceding chapters, we have explored the use of language in the *comedia* as part of a tradition that, in great measure, derives from structuralism. The present study also deals with language, but its approach is more allied with that of critics who found structuralist approaches to literature somehow lacking in terms of describing the links between language and reality. Yet the ideas proposed in this chapter are really not as alien as they might appear at first glance since at the heart of any deconstructive approach to literature lies a fundamental interest in and interrogation of language. Thus, the approach used here may differ in some respects from that of previous chapters, but many points of contact will remain the same as we examine how a specific linguistic phenomenon can influence our reading of Lope's famous drama, *Fuenteovejuna* [*The Sheep Well*].

In the past few years, those of us who study the *comedia* have increasingly found ourselves torn from the safe, comfortable approaches to the text that marked our early encounters with the great plays of the Golden Age. Interpretation in the age of poststructuralism asks us to acknowledge the problems inherent in the concept of safe readings precisely because it challenges the idea that there is a fundamental truth at the core of every literary text, leaving us with the uncomfortable thought that nothing—and certainly not language—is sacred. The ideas that every reading is ultimately a misreading, that there is afoot a way of viewing the disruptive effects of language on and in a text, and that every text posits a series of aporias or deconstructive moments when its internal logic breaks down, when the text turns in on itself, and when the secure world we knew is turned upside down, form a central aspect of contemporary theory and practice. Philosophers and literary critics have redrawn the lines that separate their respective disciplines, actively involving the reader in the process of textual explication and engaging that reader in a cocreative enterprise that, for all its use of challenging terminology, invites ever new ways of confronting the texts that we study.

No play better comes to mind after these comments about poststructuralism than *Fuenteovejuna*. Lope's drama has all the essential ingredients of a classic triumph-over-tyranny story: an evil, easily recognizable villain, a collective hero that has the underdog advantage, a pair of royal judges who make everything come out all right in the end, and a motto that becomes the symbol of the triumph of collective right over wrong, "Fuenteovejuna lo hizo" [Fuenteovejuna did it]. This motto, which simultaneously asserts the truth and challenges authority, incarnates the power of the word to make things right. Yet our study will move away from such early, safe readings in order to offer still another reading of *Fuenteovejuna*.[1] This questioning and exorcism of the traditional "right-or-wrong" reading of *Fuenteovejuna* will not, however, uncover a new truth (or core of truths) at the center of the play because deconstruction sees the nostalgia of "unity" as an unrecuperable logocentric desire. Consequently, such concepts as the primacy of truth, unity, and justice must be rejected. By focusing on certain key moments in *Fuenteovejuna*, we will examine how the play turns in on itself and turns our earlier readings upside down in a violent clash inside the text.

The violence alluded to in the title of this study is really threefold. First, the clash occurring within the fabric of the text emerges as a violent undoing of the notion that Lope's play foregrounds the triumph of good over evil, heroism over tyranny, right over wrong. As we will see, *Fuenteovejuna* offers multiple readings, some of which antithetically oppose one another.

The second level is con—or counter—textual, in that the violence in the play functions on a number of levels as a recurring motif: violence surfaces in the attack on Ciudad Real, in the violence of the Comendador's [Commander of Calatrava's] acts of aggression toward his own subjects in the village, in the villagers' corresponding violence in their assassination of the Comendador, and in the Pesquisidor's [Investigator's] torture of the villagers as a means of ascertaining the truth for Ferdinand and Isabella. The violence of the Comendador's acts of aggression toward his subjects highlights the kinds of hierarchical relationships that exist in the town. His acts of power include rape (certainly an extreme act of violence and power), robbery, and other abuses of his position as the privileged member of the hierarchy. Yet, in *Fuenteovejuna,* violence is matched with violence as the people of the village use similarly violent acts to restore order to the town. This reciprocated violence contains within itself not just the presence, but also the absence of violence, namely, the search for peace and harmony.

Finally, the violence alluded to in the title of this analysis is in the Derridean sense of a violent hierarchy, the early privileging of speech over writing, of the signified over the signifier, that is deconstructed in Derrida's reading of Saussure's *Course in General Linguistics.* Saussure had maintained in his *Course* that "the linguistic object is not both the written and the spoken forms of words; the spoken forms alone constitute the object" and that writing "exists for the sole purpose of representing" speech (23–24). Derrida aligns Saussure's theories with Western tradition:

> . . . writing, the letter, the sensible inscription, has always been considered by Western tradition as the body and matter external to the spirit, to breath, to speech, and to the logos. (*Of Grammatology* 35)

Saussure's position, which privileges speech precisely because it exists temporally in the present, is indicative of the phonocentrism of Western thought because Saussure assumed that meaning is revealed in the presence of the spoken word.

Derrida called Saussure's subordination of writing to speech a "violent hierarchy," in which "One of the two terms governs the other . . . or has the upper hand. To deconstruct the opposition, first of all, is to overturn the hierarchy at a given moment" (*Positions* 41). Derrida's deconstruction of Saussure's bias toward speech argues that speech should not hold the privileged position in the hierarchy; Derrida consequently undoes the hierarchy by inverting it, granting the privileged position to writing. Of course, after deconstructing Saussure, Derrida does not automatically embrace writing as the privileged hierarchical member. On the contrary, he views both modes as arbitrary and nonauthoritative, and he proffers an oscillating inversion of the hierarchy. The original overturning of the hierarchy is, then, just one aspect of Derrida's radical questioning of the relationship between signs and referents, between language and objects.[2]

Derrida's view of textuality as the heterogeneous, dynamic play of differences advances the idea that the text is not the repository of hidden truths or ultimate meanings and opens the way for literary critics to continue the never-to-be-finished business of constantly seeking, but never achieving, the final meaning or truth of a text. Douglas Atkins observes, "deconstruction consists of an undoing/preserving that produces ceaseless reversal, reinscription, and oscillation of hierarchical terms" (*Reading Deconstruction* 5–6). Further, notes Vincent Leitch:

> As a mode of textual theory and analysis, contemporary *deconstruction* subverts almost everything in the tradition, putting in question received ideas of the sign and language, the text, the context, the author, the reader, the role of history, the work of interpretation, and the forms of critical writing. (*Deconstructive Criticism* ix)

The deconstructive critic does not deconstruct the text in the sense of changing it, but, rather, "is forced at best to repeat the work's contradictions in a different form" (J. H. Miller, "Stevens' Rock" 333). As Paul De Man suggests, "The deconstruction is not something we have added to the text; it constituted the text in the first place. A literary text simultaneously asserts and denies the authority of its own rhetorical mode" ("Semiology and Rhetoric" 138–39). Miller pursues the relationship existing between criticism and the text:

> The activity of deconstruction already performed and then hidden in the work must be performed again in criticism. It can be performed, however, only in such a way as to be misunderstood in its turn, like the work itself, so that it has to be done over, and then again. ("Stevens' Rock" 331)

The fact that the text has, in a sense, already been deconstructed and that the critic only lays bare something that was *always already* there (J. V. Harari, "Critical Factions/Critical Fictions" 37) is a basic tenet of deconstructive criticism if, indeed, it could ever be said that deconstruction contained anything remotely resembling tenets. It is important to remember, though, that this approach to textuality is much less radical than it has sometimes been made to appear, although such concepts as the multiplicity of opposing readings, the freeplay of language, and the abolition of such a logocentric concept as truth may prove problematic to some critics.

A literary text is always related to preexisting texts; certainly, the ties between *Fuenteovejuna* and its sources could also be interrogated in a deconstructive approach to the play. The seventeenth-century drama deconstructs its primary sixteenth-century source, Francisco de Rades y Andrada's *Chronica de las tres Ordenes y Cauallerias de Santiago, Calatraua y Alcantara* (Toledo 1572), which, in a very real sense, deconstructs its source: the historical events surrounding Fuenteovejuna's murder of the Comendador, Fernán Gómez de Guzmán, in April, 1476.[3] In the case of both Rades y Andrada's *Chronica* and Lope's *Fuenteovejuna,* history is filtered through the controlling hand of a writer, who adds, deletes, and generally amends elements of preexisting interpretations.

This intertextuality can be related closely to the notion of deconstructive readings. J. Hillis Miller discusses how deconstruction functions in a text:

> The "deconstruction" which the text performs on itself and which the critic repeats is not of the superstructure of the work but of the ground on which it stands, whether that ground is history, or the social world, or the solid, extra-linguistic world of "objects," or the givenness of the generative self of the writer, his "consciousness." ("Stevens' Rock" 333–34)

Lope's deconstruction of the *Chronicle* takes place on a number of those grounds. We must remember that although *Fuenteovejuna* is based on history—and on a subsequent prosified interpretation of historical events—it is clearly a new work of art, intended by its author to be performed as a theatrical piece. It is, therefore, a product of the consciousness of Lope, of the seventeenth century, and of the extratextual realities imposed by its genre. The *Chronicle* serves as a text and as a pre-text for Lope's play and is both "preserved and undone" in *Fuenteovejuna.*[4]

It is pertinent, then, to reconsider the historical ground on which *Fuenteovejuna* stands and which Lope deconstructs.[5] There is a high percentage of correlation between the *Chronicle* and the play, as illustrated in this fragment, entitled "El hecho de Fuenteouejuna," describing the Comendador, Fernán Gómez de Guzmán:

> hizo tantos y tan grandes agrauios a los vezinos de aquel pueblo, que no pudiendo ya fuffrirlos ni difsimularlos, determinaron todos de vn confentimiẽto y voluntad alçarfe contra el y matarle. Con efta determinaciõ y furor de pueblo ayrado, con voz de Fuenteouejuna, fe juntaron vna noche del mes de Abril, del año de mill y quatrocientos y fetenta y feys, los Alcaldes, Regidores, Iufticia y Regimiẽto, cõ los otros vezinos, y cõ mano armada, entrarõ por fuerça

> en las cafas de la Encomienda mayor, donde el dicho Comendador estaua. Todos apellidauan Fuenteouejuna, Fuenteouejuna, y dezian, Viuan los Reyes don Fernando y doña Yfabel, y muerã los traydores y malos Chriftianos.

[So many times and so seriously did he offend the people of that village that they could not suffer or overlook it any longer. So they unanimously and voluntarily decided to rise against him and kill him. With the determination and fury of an angry people, with one voice, Fuenteovejuna, the town leaders, local justice, and troops, together with the other villagers, gathered one night in the month of April of 1476. They took arms and broke into the houses of the Encomienda Mayor [the Commander's estate], where the above mentioned Comendador was. They were all shouting: Fuenteovejuna! Fuenteovejuna! and they said, Long live King Ferdinand and Queen Isabella, and death to the traitors and bad Christians! (79)

Lope follows the report of this *Chronicle* fairly faithfully, even to the point of citing the words shouted by the villagers, incorporating them into the discourse of his drama. As Leo Spitzer notes:

> Lope, reading the text, dramatic in itself, of this Chronicle, must already have heard in his ears the echoes of the lines of the play he was to write and the repetition of the cries in the Chronicle "¡Fuenteouejuna!" must have suggested to him a flow of action punctuated by such ejaculations. ("A Central Theme" 290)

Yet, Lope also judiciously alters or omits other details. His description of the villagers is less pejorative than that reported in the *Chronicle,* in part because Rades y Andrada simply gives a longer list of the "cruel actions" of the people in the town.[6] Lope's abbreviation of such a list evokes a greater degree of sympathy for the collective protagonist and concomitantly generates more negative feelings toward the Comendador.

Even more importantly, however, Lope chose to omit a key phrase from the *Chronicle* in his dramatic portrayal of history. In Rades y Andrada's account, the villagers of Fuenteovejuna "quitaron las varas y cargos de jufticia a los que eftauan pueftos por efta Orden" [they took away the staff of authority and offices of justice from those who had been given them by that military Order] (80). The *Chronicle* details the villagers' request that control of the town be transferred from the Order of Calatrava to Córdoba as a result of the abuses they had suffered under the Comendador. There is a lengthy discussion of the dispute between the Order of Calatrava and Córdoba over the town, with the eventual outcome being decided in favor of the military order. Why did Lope omit this aspect of the *Chronicle* account, when, in almost every other detail, he followed it so closely? The answer lies in the extratextual world of the seventeenth-century writer, Lope de Vega. Lope's dramatic text was written at a time and for an audience that supported the monarchy; even one hundred and fifty years after the uprising, Lope could not and did not advocate unbridled rebellion and anarchy.[7] As Menéndez y Pelayo rightly noted:

> este drama, tan profundamente democrático, es también profundamente monárquico. Ambas ideas vivían juntas en el pueblo español; y en Lope, su poeta, su intérprete, tenían que ser inseparables.

> [this drama, which is so profoundly democratic, is also profoundly promonarchy. Both ideas existed simultaneously in the minds of the Spanish people; and for Lope, their poet and interpreter, these two ideas had to be inseparable.] (178)

Still, Lope's unwavering support for the monarchy and for the status quo bears directly on the strength given to the king and to his verdict at the end of the play. Although the text presents the authority of the king as unquestionable, it simultaneously interrogates that very issue, by virtue of the way his judgment is achieved.[8]

Finally, Lope's refusal to follow Rades's narration faithfully relates to the end of the play and to the judgment rendered by the Reyes Católicos [the Catholic Monarchs, Isabella and Ferdinand]. Lope alters the *Chronicle* text by having the villagers go to the court in order to explain the reasons for their actions, to "exponer una vez más la causa de su actitud rebelde contra el Comendador y de su modo de proceder al darle muerte . . . pidiendo clemencia y justicia" [to explain once more the cause of their rebellious attitude against the Comendador, and how they put him to death . . . asking for clemency and justice] (Gómez-Moriana, *Derecho de resistencia* 71). As a result of hearing the villagers' spoken (significantly, *not written*) justification, the monarchs take over the town's direct supervision. Gómez-Moriana concludes that with this action "parece resaltar en la obra de Lope su aceptación de los hechos como justos y la inocencia del pueblo" [Lope's play seems to stress that he accepted the events as justified and considered the people not guilty] (70). The issue, however, is much more complex than this conclusion suggests: the role of speech in *Fuenteovejuna* is one that relates closely to that of writing.

The intertextual hierarchies existing between the past and the present, between the sixteenth-century *Chronicle* and the seventeenth-century play, and between truth and fiction encompass the central hierarchy that is both undone and preserved in our deconstruction of the play. In Lope's play, the point at which the text appears to contradict its own rules and logic relates directly to the violent hierarchy of speech and writing. The fundamental question posed by *Fuenteovejuna* is why the play was constructed in such a manner that at the end, after the judge affirms that he has been unable to produce even a single page of written proof as to the identity of the Comendador's murderers, the king says:

> Pues no puede averiguarse
> el sucesso por escrito,
> aunque fue grave el delito,
> por fuerça ha de perdonarse.
>
> [Since it is impossible to verify / in writing what happened, / even though the crime was of a serious nature / we are forced to pardon the town.]
>
> (3.2442–45)

The king's statement raises a number of questions concerning the nature of writing and Lope's simultaneous faith in—and condemnation of—the written word as a means of establishing truth. Certainly, the value of writing was a common topic in philosophical and metaphysical debates of the Golden Age.[9] Lope enters into the debate early in the play, offering a series of interrelated motifs that finally lead us to King Ferdinand's decree at the end of act 3.

The first scene of act 2 presents a lengthy condemnation of the printing press and the written word. The *licenciado* [graduate or lawyer], Leonelo, observes:

> Mas muchos que opinión tuvieron grave,
> por imprimir sus obras la perdieron;
> tras esto, con el nombre del que sabe,
> muchos sus ignorancias imprimieron.

[But many who were held in good opinion / lost that reputation after they printed their works; / after all that, many, passing as knowledgeable, / only managed to put their own ignorance in print.]

(2.916–19)

This passage clearly suggests that the printing press had led to the publication of a great deal of banal writing. Apart from representing a popular debate within a scene filled with local color, this critique of writing would seemingly be of little importance to the development of the dramatic action were it not part of a series of allusions to the topic.[10] Writing is foregrounded again in Laurencia and Frondoso's wedding celebration. When Mengo's parody criticizes those who write bad poetry, he adds the following observation on the process:

¿No habéis visto un buñolero,
en al azeite abrasando,
pedazos de masa echando,
hasta llenarse el caldero?
Que unos le salen hinchados,
otros tuertos y mal hechos,
ya çurdos y ya derechos,
ya fritos y ya quemados.
Pues assí imagino yo
un poeta componiendo,
la materia previniendo,
que es quien la masa le dio.
Va arrojando verso aprissa
al caldero del papel,
confiado en que la miel
cubrirá la burla y risa.
Mas poniéndolo en el pecho,
apenas hay quien los tome;
tanto, que sólo los come
el mismo que los ha hecho.

[Haven't you seen a doughnut baker / throw pieces of dough / in hot oil / until the cauldron is full? / Some come out swollen / some crooked and wrong / either to the left or to the right, / either well done or burned. / That is the way I imagine / a poet when he is composing, / the way he deals with his subject, / which acts as his dough. / He starts throwing his verses in haste / to the paper cauldron, / hoping that the honey / will hide the mockery and laughter they provoke. / But when he starts offering them for sale / hardly anyone dares take one / so he who made them / ends up eating them by himself.

(2.1514–33)

Leonelo's criticism of the printing press and Mengo's attack on how bad poets "create" their works underscore a generally negative view of the written word. It would seem, then, that writing serves to validate the work of mediocre thinkers.

The principal treatment of writing, however, occurs at the end of the play, when the written word becomes the instrument for proving culpability and, therefore, arriving at the truth, for the king sends an investigator/judge to Fuenteovejuna to obtain a written indictment against the Comendador's murderers. This royal representative attempts to ascertain the truth by torturing the villagers—young and old, male and female.[11] The judge reports that without written proof the king must either kill or pardon the villagers, all three hundred of whom steadfastly maintain that "Fuentovejuna lo hizo" [Fuenteovejuna did it]. King Ferdinand then uses the ploy that, since he has no such written indictment, he can only pardon the citizens of Fuenteovejuna, and the play ends happily.

The question of truth, however, remains unresolved. The king's decision to send the judge to Fuenteovejuna is, in effect, only a postponement, a deferral of the judgment he must make at the end of the play. When that moment of reckoning arrives, however, King Ferdinand's judgment and his rendering of justice are based on a technicality that involves the written word. The play turns on the opposition of speech, in the collective voice of the people, and writing, thus producing the violent hierarchy deconstructed by Derrida and alluded to in the title of this study of *Fuenteovejuna*.

These issues of truth and justice are developed throughout the play and are constantly related to the hierarchical relationship between speech and writing. They begin to conjoin in *Fuenteovejuna*'s third act, beginning with the *junta* [meeting] of the first scene. In this eventful scene, the villagers have decided as a group that they will kill the Comendador. The *junta*, however, is a central aspect of the issues that are raised in a deconstructive reading of the play. Geoffrey W. Ribbans's summary is a perfect recapitulation of the scene:

The five active participants in the *junta* all have different viewpoints, and are skilfully handled to make them as widely representative as possible. Esteban, the most offended against of them all, is the most impassioned; he is impatient because of the others' delay, loses control of himself, and shouts out for action. Juan Rojo and the Regidor each make a moderate suggestion—to send an appeal to the Catholic Monarchs and to abandon the town respectively—but when these are rejected they get heated—Mengo warns the meeting that they are making too much noise—and propose attacking and killing the Comendador. Only Barrildo and, especially, Mengo continue to advise caution:

> *Mengo.* Mirad, señores,
> que vais en estas cosas con recelo.
> Puesto que por los simples labradores
> estoy aquí que más injurias pasan,
> más cuerdo represento sus temores.
>
> [*Mengo.* Gentlemen, be careful / and treat these matters with caution. / Since I am here representing the simple peasants, / the ones who were the most offended, / I'm the one to speak for their fears.]
>
> The whole episode seems to me to show how passion takes hold of these simple peasants, unused to such weighty issues, and causes such abrupt changes of position. ("Meaning and Structure" 165)

Laurencia joins this meeting and exhorts the males to act, and the earlier moderate *junta* dissolves into a mob seeking collective vengeance:

> *Mengo.* Juntad el pueblo a una voz;
> que todos están conformes
> en que los tiranos mueran.
>
> [*Mengo.* Join the people in one single voice: / all are agreed / that the tyrants must die.]
>
> (3.1806–8)

The villagers have moved from passivity to action. Both reason and passion have led to their decision to kill the Comendador, but, even more importantly, they have determined that his death at their hands is their only real option.

Two aspects of this decision are important. First, the decision-making scenes are examples of the few places in which Lope adds significantly to the *Chronica:* both the *junta* and the scenes in which Laurencia attacks the men for their cowardice are expanded (or, in the case of Laurencia, added) to heighten the dramatic tension. We can see how Lope has chosen to move away from the historical sources that have been governing his reading. Further, these scenes lie at the heart of the problem of reconciling truth and justice in the play. The people of the town decide that they will act collectively to kill their tyrant. Yet, their unanimity of purpose does not lend any greater degree of moral acceptability to their actions.[12] Lope leaves us with several questions: does the decision to kill the Comendador represent an attempt to act on their desire for vengeance, or is it an attempt to render justice? If the second is true, is their action legal—and is that issue pertinent?[13]

Finally, we must ask if their action is just—right—in terms not of motivation, but of style. Ribbans notes the contradiction. Although the Comendador "richly deserves his ignominious end," nevertheless:

> from the other point of view, the villagers are also at fault. They are provoked beyond all control of reason to a "furor maldito y rabioso," and show all the blind and undisciplined symptoms of a popular rising; the women forget their true nature and attempt to act as men; the rebels refuse to listen to Fernán Gómez's conciliatory offer, and Frondoso when released joins the attackers; above all a nobleman is butchered like a common criminal and his body treated with ignominy and contempt. ("Meaning and Structure" 166–67)

While Ribbans might well be challenged on some aspects of his conclusion (notably his comments regarding the women of the town and, particularly, those dealing with Frondoso), he has, nonetheless, centered on the essence of the issue of justice in the play. The issue will be complicated much further as the play progresses toward its climax because the collectivity of action will extend to the level of the villagers' defense and to the means chosen to determine their culpability and punishment.

The citizens of Fuenteovejuna do not deny their guilt. In fact, they first rehearse their confessions and justifications and then carry them out, even under torture, when the king's investigator arrives to determine the truth. Yet, the truth of the utterance "Fuenteovejuna lo hizo" [Fuenteovejuna did it] is suspect. The women are not even in the room when the Comendador is killed, and all of the men could not have struck the mortal blow simultaneously:

> Appropriately, the Comendador is killed off-stage, and no one villager can be singled out as his killer. . . . Esteban cries, "¡Muere, traidor Comendador!" just before the Comendador's dying speech,

> but the audience is no more sure of anything than is the judge who comes to investigate. (Ribbans, "Meaning and Structure" 167)

The notion at work here is that of collective intention and, consequently, collective culpability, a type of moral complicity based on the battle cry, "todos a una" [all for one and one for all]. Nevertheless, on a literal level, Fuenteovejuna did not do it; in addition, the villagers' response does not convey sufficient information to offer any sort of ultimate proof. The play, then, proposes two levels of truth—one moral and metaphoric and the other literal—a fact that bestows an even greater degree of importance on the quest for truth initiated by the king. Ironically, the king's judgment ignores both the literal and moral levels just described in favor of a response that chooses expediency over truthfulness and keeps speech as the privileged member of the violent hierarchy.

The prevailing critical interpretation of the end of the play suggests that the king's pardon of the villagers is an example of the triumph of justice.[14] Ribbans proclaims:

> Their loyalty and steadfastness together seem to me, in Lope's conception, to exculpate their fault: they deserve the pardon they receive in the final scene. On the other hand, the torture is not unjust, as rebellion merits punishment. (168)

We are still left, however, with the problem of reconciling justice and truth. This problem is complicated further in the respective appeals of Flores and the villagers to the king. The two oral reports of what happened are completely contradictory. Flores insists that the villagers acted without just cause, that they mistreated the Comendador's corpse and looted his house, and, in general, merited an extreme sort of punishment.[15] The villagers, however, maintain that the Comendador abused his rank and power, robbed them, and treated the village women as his personal sexual objects. We are left with two completely contradictory interpretations of the truth, presented orally, and requiring two totally different reactions in terms of the justice issue. Each reading contains elements that cannot be proven conclusively within the text of the play, but certainly, each must contain a small element of truth: both the villagers and the Comendador do act atrociously. Although the villagers' motivation may be justified, neither side is totally without blame in a society whose values include the medieval notion of *derecho de pernada* [*droit du seigneur,* including a lord's right to possess all women in his domain before they marry]. If we cannot prove who is right, if we intuit that both sides share at least a small part of the blame for the situation, we must return again to the question of how Lope links justice to truth.

In seeking the truth so that he can deliver a just judgment, King Ferdinand has attempted to privilege writing over speech, but no one—including his personal inquisitor—can produce the written corroboration he requires. This corroboration would be in the form of a written repetition of the villagers' oral confession, a material object that would serve to formalize and legitimize the spoken word. The power of the written word, of course, has been witnessed through the centuries and can be traced back within the Judeo-Christian tradition to the ultimate word of God in the Bible. Certainly, God's earthly envoy in fifteenth-century Spain, King Ferdinand, clings to the notion that written confirmation of culpability is a necessary ingredient for determining truth and meting out justice.

In contrast, the villagers seem to privilege speech over writing. By insisting upon their communal affirmation that "Fuenteovejuna lo hizo"—and by insisting that those words, and only those words, will be uttered to the judge—they leave the judge with no real confession to reproduce in writing precisely because their words offer no explanatory details. Since, for Derrida, the linguistic sign reveals the play of presence and absence, we may extend the metaphor to see that the presence of the words "Fuenteovejuna lo hizo" also suggests the absence of utterances explaining who really struck the mortal blow, how the Comendador was killed, how many people were in the room at the time of his death, etc. By focusing on the endless repetition of these exact words (and nothing more), the villagers have left the judge with nothing to report in writing; he is unable to ascertain the whole truth of the situation. That which cannot be inscribed cannot produce a verdict (that which is "truly said"). In other words, the investigator's failure to provide the monarchs with written corroboration of guilt denies them the means by which they can verify the truth.

Still, while the villagers do not give the judge enough data to write his report, they do go to the king in order to report directly—and orally. In the end, there is a conflict (or hierarchy) between the power of the king (related to God, law, authority, truth, and country) and the power of the collective (related to believers, justice, vengeance, rural village, etc.). This conflict underlines the problem of the individual ruler versus the collective will, examining how the use of power can restore unity and harmony. Teresa Kirschner sees this conclusion as a triumph of the collective will:

> El triunfo de Fuenteovejuna no sale del perdón real (ya que no son perdonados técnicamente), sino que radica en haber *forzado* incluso a los Reyes a que se les tome como una unidad, en su fuerza del querer colectivo.

> [The triumph of Fuenteovejuna does not result from a royal pardon (technically, they are not pardoned) but lies in their having *forced* everyone, including the monarchs, to consider them as a unit, to recognize their force as collective will.] (*El protagonista* 140)

What happens in *Fuenteovejuna* is that the villagers have taken their version of truth and justice, affirmed it, and made it real through the solidarity of group action. The cathartic, communal confession embodied in the words "Fuenteovejuna lo hizo" both proclaims guilt and simultaneously allows for a type of "justice" that, in effect, negates the force of those same spoken words. Lope has given us a series of indications that justice, inherently linked to the truth and the "Word," is an illusory concept at best. The truth value of the spoken word is undercut by a lack of written corroborating evidence, a written transcription that is a repetition of the oral speech act. In *Fuenteovejuna,* speech cannot be repeated in writing; and since the nature of writing is that it is always repeatable, we are left with a double negation of truth, a value that should be eminently reiterable. The result is a judgment that does not derive from the truth and that leaves us with unanswered questions from a text that exhibits the concurrent undoing and preserving of authorial discourse. The king's decision is, then, equivocal, because while he affirms his power as final arbiter, he also demonstrates his powerlessness with the arbitrary reasoning upon which he has based his pardon.

Lope has given early indications of his pervasive distrust of writing. The play's conclusion, incarnate in the king's judgment, underscores the contradictions and equivocations that exist between that which is spoken and that which is written. Truth and justice remain antithetically opposed in this curious interplay of speech and writing in which the dramatic text turns in on itself. Terry Eagleton observes that with deconstruction, literary criticism "becomes an ironic, uneasy business, an unsettling venture into the inner void of the text which lays bare the illusoriness of meaning, the impossibility of truth, and the deceitful guiles of all disourse" (*Literary Theory* 146). Given that definition, it would appear that *Fuenteovejuna* is a drama that has been waiting for a deconstructive critic to explore the indeterminacy of discourse in the play.

Interestingly, Lope reflects this equivocal posture with regard to language in a letter to the duke of Sessa, in which he describes the tension inherently embodied in all discourse:

> Y sobre todo quento con la moderación de las palabras; que palabras son las flechas de los moros de Pelayo, que se vuelven con los dueños, y esto hacesse facilmente y remediasse con dificultad.

> [And above all, I observe moderation with my words; words are like the arrows of King Pelayo's Moors, which turned themselves against their owners, and this is easy do to, yet more difficult to correct.] (42f.)

This letter lays bare the conflict at the heart of the violent hierarchy of discourse—both spoken and written—upon which this text turns. As a matter of fact, Lope seems well aware of the system of differences that precludes facile attempts to arrive at the play's meaning.

In a similar context, a number of contemporary critics have come to the conclusion that Calderón's honor dramas deconstruct the honor code. As Henryk Ziomek notes, "According to new explanations, the Calderonian honor plays . . . are actually theses arguing against the old code of honor" (*History* 143). I would maintain that a similar situation exists with *Fuenteovejuna.* As we delve deeper into the fabric of Lope's text, we find something that was already inscribed there: a radical questioning of referential language, of how spoken and written discourse functions.[16] In the presence of speech and the absence of writing, we see the play of difference and the estrangement of language from the world, the latter realized in the estrangement of the signifier from the signified (Rifelj, "Deconstruction Workers" 4). There is, then, a vital point in the play where we see reaffirmed the impossibility of finding a system that adequately explains that text. That place, marked by the king's decision to pardon the villagers because of a lack of written confirmation—and despite their verbal confession—curiously preserves *and* undoes Derrida's deconstruction of Saussure. In one sense, Lope's violent hierarchy maintains the Saussurian privileging of speech over writing, but it also undermines the logocentric notion that *Fuenteovejuna* presents the triumph of truth and justice. As such, we are confronted by a text that "simultaneously asserts and denies the authority of its rhetorical mode" (De Man, "Semiology and Rhetoric" 138–39).

Lope's *Fuenteovejuna* therefore exposes the violent hierarchies of speech and writing, of the assertion and denial of textual authority, of past readings and present deconstructions. Consequently, it subverts the type of privileged status it formerly enjoyed when the drama seemed the quintessential model of justifiable action and reasoned response. As we have seen, a deconstructive approach to the play interrogates this model, leaving the reader/spectator with the uncomfortable feeling that truth and justice are not, and cannot be, what they once were.

7

Literary History, Literary Theory, and *Cada uno para sí:* The Dramatist as Reader and Rewriter of His Own Text

I see the challenge to literary studies of taking up once again the problem of literary history.

—H. R. Jauss

As we have seen in the preceding chapters of this study, in recent years, newer critical approaches and theoretical models have emerged in the academic marketplace and have changed forever the ways that we study Golden Age drama. *Comedia* scholars have explored ways of examining dramatic texts that have both complemented and, occasionally, confounded historical or New Critical readings of Golden Age theater. The real point here is that the theories posited since the 1940s—and especially since the 1960s—by American and European critics have served an invaluable function when used as tools for allowing us to "see anew" the plays that we study, and when they permit the "tracing of a path along textual strata in order to stir up and expose forgotten and dormant sediments of meaning which have accumulated and settled into the text's fabric" (Harari, "Critical Factions/Critical Fictions" 37). I would like to suggest, however, that our enthusiasm for theory need not—and should not—obscure either the essence of the text itself, or the valuable work of the historical and textual scholars who have given us the texts themselves and the contexts from which they derive. In that spirit, the present study will reconsider some of the aspects of textual production and representation that we sometimes take for granted, will deal with some theoretical issues that can help illuminate the nature of response, and will examine how the *comedia* has succeeded in standing the test of time. These concepts, fundamentally related to the topics of production, reception, and response, link the past with the present and the dramatist with his public. Ultimately, our analysis of textual transmission will lead us back to a specific play, Calderón's *Cada uno para sí [Every Man for Himself],* and to the ways that one dramatic text can illustrate the complex relationship existing among the author, the text, the audience, language, and literary history.

The transmission of the text from the pen of the writer to its audience was governed by numerous factors. Even when dramatists were supported by wealthy or royal patrons, their plays were not instantaneously performed onstage. Moreover, once plays were sold to acting companies, they most often left the dramatists' hands forever. The *autores de comedias* [producers/directors/stage managers of Golden Age plays] often altered scripts at will, making changes to suit their own esthetic tastes or to reflect performance needs. Sections of plays were often cut, eliminating scenes that were difficult to stage; furthermore, when they were cut, those cuts tended to be made at the end of a play (Greer, "Calderón" 79). Key parts were sometimes expanded to highlight the talents of certain members of the acting company. In addition, factors such as sketchy stage directions in most scripts promoted these types of textual alterations, since the company would be trying to create an actual performance text that would be used in the near future.

Other staging factors might surface only during the rehearsal of the play as it was being prepared for performance. D. W. Cruickshank discusses these last possibilities in the introduction to his edition of *En la vida todo es verdad y todo mentira [In Life, Everything Is Both True and False],* noting that the *autor de comedias* in possession of that play might have read it, found it too long, and asked Calderón to shorten it by focusing his cuts on the *gracioso* parts, since this same *autor* was also the actor who played the *gracioso* and was extremely busy with other projects at that time (xvi–xvii). Cruickshank adds two other related points of interest: first, "Calderón was known to have been in the habit of attending rehearsals" (xvii); in addition:

> In normal circumstances, an author had no rights after he had sold his play to the company manager, but Calderón, who would already have had a reputation for grumbling at the mutilation of his plays, would most likely have been present at the royal performance, so the *autor de comedias* might well have found himself in trouble had he made any unauthorized cuts. (xvi)

The plays passed through even more hands at the level of production: managers needed multiple copies of the scripts in order to stage the plays, so they had a number of scribal copies made by copyists appointed by or including the *apuntador* [prompter]. Every hand through which the text passed increased the likelihood that alterations would be made in the text, for many copyists also felt free to "improve" upon the plays that they copied. Others altered the original manuscripts simply because scribal copying invites error; it is painstaking work, often with difficult handwriting, and the monotony of the task sometimes led to the production of copies that differed significantly from the originals.

Similar problems were faced when *comedias* were printed, which generally occurred after they had served their purpose as performance texts for the commercial stage. Again, the plays passed through a great number of hands; editors and copyists compounded the problems of textual authority, often consciously and deliberately. Calderón complained about the large numbers of plays that were incorrectly attributed to him by editors who had anthologized plays he had not written, although they had used his name to attract a wider readership. In the prologue to the *Cuarta parte [Fourth Part* or *Collection]* (1672), Calderón bemoaned the sorry state of published editions, complaining that even the plays that were his own were "llenas de erratas, y por el ahorro del papel, aun no cabales (pues donde acada el pliego, acaba la Iornada, y donde acaba el cuaderno, acaba la Comedia)" [full of errors, and to save paper, not without defects, (since where the page ends, the act ends, and where the book ends, the entire play ends)] (fqq2 verso). Finally, even the layout of the words on paper affected textual transmission: stage directions and scenes at the ends of acts were frequently cut in order to save paper, especially in *suelta* [loose or separate] editions (Varey, "Staging" 155).

Lope also raised his voice in opposition to the practice. Arnold Reichenberger tells us that in the prologue to *Parte* XVII:

> Lope invents two lawsuits by the allegorical character *El teatro* against the booksellers. The booksellers win each time because they prove that once the playwrights are paid they no longer have any rights at all to their plays. There exists complete chaos: the *autores* steal the plays from each other or they sell them to the towns which need them for their festivities. They insert other verses where it pleases them, or they steal or buy these from playwrights' secretaries. Lope ends by complaining that the most harmful thing for an author is to have his *comedias* printed. The poet cannot control the publication—especially when he never even kept a copy of his work. (9–10)

Yet, even more filters could—and did—affect textual transmission. The *grandes memorias* ["great memories," those who memorized plays] or *memoriones,* who sat through several performances and wrote down what they remembered for booksellers or rural *autores,* could hardly be counted upon to aid any attempts at establishing textual authority. José Ruano de la Haza has discussed the profundity of the changes wrought when a *memorión* collaborated with an adapter to produce a rehash of Lope de Vega's *Peribáñez* for a rural audience. The existence of the *memorión* complicated an already complex situation because the changes he wrought produced a new text, one that differed considerably from Lope's original, but that better met the performance needs of that particular type of audience.[1]

Both printed and stage versions of *comedia* texts were also affected by yet another factor: the presence of official censors, who often objected to parts of a play found to be offensive and who consequently served to halt the forward movement of the play from author to public. Although most plays conformed to official requirements, E. M. Wilson reminds us that "the censors sometimes objected to allusions that seemed profane or irreverent . . . to what seemed immoral or scandalous . . . or heretical" ("Calderón and the Stage Censor" 182). Further, "There seems to exist a possible correlation between the severity of the censorship and the theatrical legislation of the seventeenth century" (182). In 1615, the Consejo de Castilla *[Council of Castille]* detailed the rules regarding the censorship of performances. Before the scripts were given to the actors, they were to be sent to the official censor for approval, since:

> sin esta licencia no se representen ni se hagan, el cual las censurará, no permitiendo cosa lasciva ni deshonesta, ni malsonante ni en daño de otros, ni de materia que no convenga que salga en público.

[without this license, they may not be performed. The censor must censor them, and he should not allow lewdness, indecency, profanity or things that may be harmful to others, nor material that should not be made public.] (Wilson 165)

Censors also showed up on the first day a work was performed in order to make certain that their proscriptions had been observed.

Yet, by 1644, restrictions had tightened even more, and only certain types of plays were permitted to be performed, including "historias de vidas de santos" [stories about the saints' lives] and other

> materias de buen exemplo, formándose de vidas y muertes exemplares, de hazañas valerosas; de gobiernos políticos, que todo esto fuese *sin mezcla de amores;* que para conseguirlo se prohibiesen casi todas las que hasta entonces se habían representado, especialmente los libros de Lope de Vega, que tanto daño habían hecho en las costumbres.

> [matters of good example, made out of exemplary lives and deaths, courageous deeds, examples of good government, and all this should be *without mixing in love stories,* and in order to do this, they should ban almost all the ones performed up to that date, especially the books by Lope de Vega, which had done so much harm to public morality.] (Wilson 165)

Ecclesiastical censorship was particularly strong in the years before and after the closing of the theaters in the late 1640s, although the evidence given by Wilson suggests that there was a certain amount of disagreement even among the censors as to what material should be judged objectionable. The theater was, of course, a special case for censorship because of its immediacy and oral nature: "the word spoken in public was always thought to be more scandalous than what might quite legitimately be read in private" (Wilson 170). Consequently, the censor played an important role in the development and transmission of the *comedia* within Spain, both through direct alterations of dramatic texts and by means of the psychological imperative that censorship created for dramatists who knew that their works would receive careful scrutiny.

The above discussion assumes that textual transmission occurred only in Spain and in the Spanish language. As scholars such as Martin Franzbach and Henry Sullivan have noted with regard to Calderón, dramatic texts also passed throughout Europe (not to mention the New World) in numerous printed versions, translations, and adaptations.[2] The complexity of the issue of transmission is, therefore, further highlighted by the addition of even more layers of filters. Translators add yet another step in the process, and foreign adaptations necessarily underscore the notion that each new director or editor would often modify the original text to reflect the literary, cultural, philosphical, and theatrical contexts of his own country, of his own age, and for his own audience.

What are, then, the consequences of *comedia* texts having such large numbers of filters? As William F. Hunter observes, "in transmission the rare and the original are eliminated or conventionalized, jokes and puns vanish, learned or unfamiliar references are distorted" ("Editing Texts" 30). Every hand that touches the text increases the likelihood that such corruption will occur and that we will be even further distanced from the author's original. Still, the modifications that result from so many filters form part of the history and, indeed, the entire temporal existence of the text. Hunter reminds us that

> while we always like to know "what the author wrote and meant," in a historical perspective the public life of a work after it leaves the privacy of the author's desk is just as important, and even more so. (34)

Finally, as part of this historical perspective, it is important to note that dramatists themselves sometimes—although not frequently—returned to their own texts at a later date, revising their plays for personal reasons or in collaboration with the *autores de comedias*. Such textual reworking gives us a great deal of information about readers, writers, and copyists. Margaret Rich Greer observes that "An examination of a number of autograph or partly autograph manuscripts in the Biblioteca Nacional reveals that a majority of these manuscripts show evidence of substantial alteration at the end of one or more acts" ("Calderón" 75–76). The external, pragmatic factors affecting the alterations that have been described above offer a number of reasons for such textual modification. In addition, these factors might have been complemented by esthetic motivations. Greer reminds us that "Calderón . . . viewed endings as the climax of a work of art, as that which gave shape to the whole and therefore [he] dedicated particular attention to them" (79).

Consequently, it would follow that given the opportunity to rework one of his own texts, Calderón might have chosen to focus on its ending, which is precisely the case of *Cada uno para sí,* a *comedia de capa y espada* [cloak and sword play] that was probably first written between 1652–1653[3] and whose ending was then reworked years after its composition. In the Biblioteca National's partly autograph manuscript of *Cada uno para sí,* Calderón's hand appears as one of the five copyists of the text. He returned to the script owned at that time by an acting company and participated in its revision by changing the third act of the play, altering some scenes, deleting others, and adding an entirely new one. In that sense, Calderón was not only the writer, but later the reader and rewriter of his own text.

The case in point could be singled out simply because it was rather unusual for dramatists to return to their works and to edit them in future years. It is further marked, however, because of the curious twist described above: when a writer comes back to his own work after the passage of time, his relationship with the text will have changed dramatically and fundamentally. Calderón's rereading will, by definition, be a very different reading. It is here, in the clash between the reader, the writer, and the text, that we can attempt to illuminate the links between the seventeenth and the twentieth centuries, between text and interpretation, and between language and history, theory and practice.

Ruano de la Haza has edited *Cada uno para sí* in an eclectic edition that probably reflects Calderón's final version of the play, which the dramatist created when he returned to his text some fifteen to twenty years after its composition.[4] The manuscript found in the Biblioteca Nacional was "probably the main manuscript of a play belonging to a theatrical company" (Ruano 4), in this case, that of Antonio de Escamilla, one of the five copyists of the play and an important theatrical figure of the time—an actor famous for playing *gracioso* roles, an *autor,* and a writer of *entremeses* [comic interludes] and *fines de fiesta* [short dramatic pieces performed at the end of a longer play]. Escamilla compiled the text of the play, using the first two acts of the *princeps* edition of 1661, that is, the *Parte XV* of the *Comedias escogidas [Selected Plays],* as the source of the first two acts of his performance script. These acts show two different hands; the copyists were probably members of Escamilla's company (Ruano 19). Unfortunately, the third act of the first edition was extremely corrupt so Escamilla had to recreate the third act of his compiled performance text from Calderón's revision of an earlier copy. Sometime before the first printed edition appeared in 1661, another copyist, Sebastián de Alarcón, had participated in copying the third act of *Cada uno.* Ruano speculates that after the corrupt *princeps* edition appeared, Calderón was moved to return to his text in order to revise it, but since he had sold the play to an *autor,* he no longer had any right of ownership. Calderón subsequently had to turn to the best available copy of his text—the copy done by Sebastián de Alarcón. Alarcón had copied at least two other plays that Calderón later used as sources for his revisions (Ruano 18), so the precedent had clearly been established.

We can see, then, that the principal reason why Calderón would want to modify the third act of his play is directly linked to the corrupt version that appeared in the *princeps* edition. Calderón rightly complained about the poor quality of printed editions of his plays. In this early edition, countless errors appeared in the first two acts, and the third act was only half as long as it should have been. Over four hundred verses were left out, and the act even began abruptly in the middle of a scene. "The editors of the *princeps* edition were trying to present a shorter, albeit clumsily edited, version of the third act of *Cada uno*" (Ruano 43), precisely the criticism Calderón had leveled at the printers of his plays in the quotation cited earlier. Consequently, Calderón, spurred on by the corrupt version of the *princeps* edition, used Alarcón's copy to rewrite act 3 of *Cada uno*. He followed Alarcón's text as long as possible, leaving much of it the same, but he made a number of changes as well. Calderón altered several scenes at the end of the play, eliminating one, modifying another, cutting several of the *gracioso's* lines and tightening the comic quality of the *gracioso* subplot. A specific example can help to illustrate the changes Calderón wrought.

The dramatist tightened the construction of his plot by eliminating a scene prior to the denouement and by changing the setting of the latter. In the original version, an extra scene intervenes between the climactic scene involving a triple duel and the play's denouement: the three gallants arrive at the *dama*'s [female lead's] house, declare their love, and hide from subsequent visitors. The comic quality of the scene resides in the number of suitors crowded into a small space, each hiding from one another, until the fathers finally arrive and the plot complication is resolved. This version, however, emphasizes the female characters more than the males; in his revision, Calderón eliminates the scene and the plot proceeds from the point at which the duel ends. Ruano de la Haza suggests that the primitive version was recast because it was weak in terms of character motivation, style, and situation (355):

> Calderón, however, soon realized that this was not the central point of the play. Both thematically and structurally, the climactic scene of the play is the triple duel scene. It is here that all the triangles of the main plot are seen to amalgamate into one. . . . Any scene placed between the triple duel scene and the dénouement would then constitute an anticlimax.
>
> Consequently, the scene of the "crowded room" had to be eliminated, the triple duel scene shifted to its rightful place, and a new scene added. . . . (356)

As this example and Ruano's analysis illustrate, it might be argued that Calderón's rewriting of act 3 of *Cada uno para sí* proffers a more refined and structurally tighter version of what must be the primitive version of his play, Alarcón's copy of a lost original.

Calderón probably returned to his text between 1665–1670, perhaps because the court theaters were closed at that time, and he was free to write. Furthermore, based on Cruickshank's useful article on Calderón's handwriting, we can conclude that this time frame for the revision of his text matches the characteristics of Calderón's handwriting style found in the manuscript. Three factors typify the elements of Calderón's handwriting at that time: the placement of speakers' names on new lines (which occurred after 1652), Calderón's progression toward regular word division, and most importantly, his manner of forming the letters f, b, p, and t, and the word "el." Ruano's analysis of these elements leads to the conclusion that Calderón returned to his play between fifteen and twenty years after its original composition (27).

As we can see, the situation became increasingly complicated as the text passed through large numbers of hands and filters. Actually, the dramatist, the *autor de comedias,* and the copyists, typesetters, censors, and editors all contributed to the process of textual transmission. In addition, some of these filters and transmitters functioned on multiple levels. An *autor* such as Escamilla was interested not only in making a copy of *Cada uno para sí,* but also in making a performance copy of the text. As an actor and as manager of his theatrical company, Escamilla was often more concerned with resolving staging problems than with dealing with issues of textual authority. This reader of Calderón's play practiced interpretation by making a number of changes in the text that he bought and then altered to fit performance requirements.

Yet Calderón's relationship with his own play is even more interesting. When writers become readers—and then rewriters—of their own texts, they also become part of a process that multiplies and reverses such communicative models as that of Roman Jakobson. Here, the process of transmitting a message from the sender to the receiver is turned back on itself. The receiver of the message, Calderón himself, becomes involved in a hermeneutic process that actualizes the text's meaning in a very concrete way. When that reader decides to intervene a second time in the writing process, he *acts* upon the text by transforming that object into a new repository of meanings. This is a step beyond the notion that all texts allow for an almost limitless number of possible readings. How Calderón received his own text, then, becomes an essential part of our examination of the writing, reading, and rewriting process that marks the production of *Cada uno para sí.*

* * *

Reception theory, particularly as developed by Hans Robert Jauss at the end of the turbulent period of the 1960s in Germany, became most widely known through his influential essay, "Literary History as a Challenge to Literary Theory" (reworked in a modified version in *Toward an Aesthetic of Reception*). Jauss tried to exact a compromise between Marxist, historical views of literature and the text-oriented approach of the Formalist school. He made famous Gadamer's notions that the meaning of the text is part of an historically evolving process and that textual interpretaion is realized as a dialogue between past and present.

In that sense, the idea of a horizon of expectations helps to explain literary reception and interpretation. The horizon of expectations includes the cultural, literary, and historical criteria that readers use when they react to texts in any given moment in history; it constitutes the "sum total of reactions, prejudgments, verbal and other behavior that greet a work upon its appearance" (*Aesthetic Experience* xii). A text may either confirm or disappoint the expectations of the reader. The disappointment of expectations leads to the creation of esthetic distance and a continual shifting or change of horizons as new nexts appear (*Toward an Aesthetic* 25).

Jauss builds upon and greatly modifies his earlier theories in such later works as *Aesthetic Experience and Literary Hermeneutics.* In this more recent volume, Jauss distinguishes various categories of esthetic reception and challenges literary hermeneutics to "shed light on the actual process through which the effect and significance of the text concretizes itself for the present reader," and further, to "reconstruct the historical process in which readers have received and interpreted the text at different times and in different ways" (xxix). Jauss focuses on "the dynamic process of production and reception, of author, work and public" (xxx–xxxi), showing us how the entire esthetic experience helps us to "see anew," to interpret texts in a way that allows us to recuperate lost time (10).[5]

Jauss's ideas on the nature of esthetic reception imply an active relationship between the writer, the reader, and the text, an ongoing series of questions and answers revealing constantly changing horizons of expectations. Jauss explains how this relationship functions:

> The reconstruction of the horizon of expectations, in the face of which a work was created and received in the past, enables one . . . to pose questions that the text gave an answer to, and thereby to discover how the contemporary reader could have viewed and understood the work. *(Toward an Aesthetic* 28)

Using this concept as a model, we may then speculate about the relationship between Calderón as writer and as reader of his play. While it should be noted that Jauss seems to be examining literary history in more generalized terms, his ideas on changing horizons of expectations work perfectly with the temporal frame that delineates Calderón's confrontation with his own text. The fifteen-to-twenty years between the composition of *Cada uno* and its revision are crucial to Calderón's development as a writer. His own history—as well as the entire changing social and cultural history of Spain—has given him a new perspective from which to receive and judge his play. He has matured as a writer and, in the interim, has begun writing very different types of theatrical texts. His experiences with the printers of his plays have been less than positive, and he returns to his text motiviated by a need to restore the authorial integrity lost by the printers of the *princeps* edition. The horizon of expectations with which Calderón greets his play after such a long period of time will, then, be fundamentally different from that of his own earlier readings of the play. The time shift between the original reading/writing process and that occurring so many years later mandates a profoundly different approach to the text. We may only be able to speculate on the reasons motivating Calderón's editorial revisions, but we can certainly look at the reading and writing of the play as representative of a temporally evolving process, one that translates changing receptions into concomitantly changing responses.

A related case of reception merits our consideration. A late eighteenth-century reader/spectator of *Cada uno* reviewed the play from within the horizon of expectations of his own era, complaining about the play's excessive amount of physical and temporal movement and about its confusing plot, although it should be noted that the critic enjoyed the "ingeniosa y graciosa solución de tantas confusiones" [witty and charming solution to so much confusion] (Ruano 108). Now, this neoclassical reading of *Cada uno* illustrates Jauss's notion of esthetic reception, as readers in later periods confront texts from the perspective of their own cultural and historical horizons of expectations. It also reminds us of how Calderón modified his text fifteen to twenty years after he wrote it. Since that revision dealt precisely with the "ingeniosa y graciosa solución" of the *enredo* [tangled plot] described by this eighteenth-century critic, a return to the title, theme, and ending of *Cada uno para sí* may help to illustrate the links between Jauss's theories and Calderón's practice.

The title of this cloak and sword play conveys the notion that in the real world it's "every man for himself." This theme operates on all levels of the plot, in which, "in matters of love, money, and social honor, everyone acts *cada uno para sí*" (Ruano 128). In typical *comedia* fashion, the characters read every situation incorrectly, creating confusion and exhibiting jealousy and deception in the process, all of which leads to the famous triple duel scene at the end. Ruano rightly concludes that Calderón only intended that the moral of the title be taken on a superficial (ironic) level, and that the best reading of *Cada uno* is that Calderón decried this kind of egotistical view of the world. What becomes significant is that we are faced again with the questions of reading and reception. The characters misread the words of other characters, thereby allowing a great deal of confusion and comic irony to operate on a textual level. In addition, we have seen that Calderón himself gave us his own contradictory readings of the title, theme, and moral of the play. His reading of the end of the third act led to the revision that allowed the irony described above to be articulated more clearly. In fact, it could be argued that *Cada un para sí* is a play about readings and misreadings, about readers, interpreters, and writers. We might then conclude that the twentieth-century theorist may help to explain just a bit better the horizon of expectations of the seventeenth-century dramatist.

* * *

Up to this point, we have analyzed reception and response in terms of Jauss's ideas regarding literary history, applied on a smaller scale to Calderón's changing responses to his own text. This analysis, however, will extend the analogy even further to the level of the relationships between and among the characters of the play. In other words, we will use Jauss's ideas about the relationship between writers, texts, and audiences not only as a metaphor for what happens with Calderón's two versions of his play, but for what happens inside the text. Reception theory, by developing the notion of the horizon, deals with the burden of the past on present readings. The links between the reading and writing processes and changing horizons of expectations also delineate the dramatic action of *Cada uno*.

Since the theater thrives on conflict, on postponing resolution until the end, and on achieving these goals through the use of blocking characters and situations, we can see how Jauss's ideas could operate on a textual level. We have discussed previously the idea that the *comedia* depends upon willed ambiguity and linguistic misfiring to create conflict. On the levels of its characters and the dramatic action, the *comedia* requires that many of its characters "read" incorrectly; their false assumptions, misinterpretations, and unproven allegations fuel the fires of the dramatic conflict. The *comedia* allows for the resolution of such (mis)readings at the character level in the conventionalized endings that characterize the genre.

In *Cada uno* as, of course, in most cloak and sword plays, it could be argued that the entire drama is about characters reading and misreading the words of other characters, that is, about reception and response, about horizons of expectations that change throughout the course of the play. It is obvious here that I have used Jauss's theories of *esthetic* reception in a specific way, that is, in terms of *linguistic* reception and response, although I would certainly acknowledge the importance of the play's physical action in combination with its dramatic discourse to describe how reception and response function in the fully integrated theatrical experience.

In this particular play, Calderón sets up a situation in which the principal *galán* [gallant, male lead], Don Félix, fearing that his beloved Doña Leonor has betrayed him, and refusing to believe her protestations of innocence, discovers only at the end of the play that her two other suitors are his own best friends, although he also learns that Leonor had never really loved the other men at all. The situation is further complicated because the two friends, Don Carlos and Don Enrique, have become enmeshed in a tangled question of honor dealing with past injuries, the love of yet another woman, Leonor's cousin, Violante, and Enrique's obligation to gather the information that Carlos needs to become a knight of Santiago. All five of these principal characters, then, are involved in conflicts arising from matters of love (requited and unrequited), money, friendship, family loyalty, and honor. Félix's refusal to believe in Leonor's innocence leads to the interweaving of these conflicts until, at the end, the fathers of the two women stop the three men from fighting a triple duel, unravel the complicated knot of relationships, and pair their daughters off: Doña Leonor will marry Don Félix, and Doña Violante will marry Don Carlos, while Don Enrique is left without a bride.

Calderón has created a plot rife with misunderstandings (i.e., misreadings of intentions) that foregrounds and defers all attempts at resolution and reconciliation. Throughout the play, Félix cannot guess the identity of the mystery woman who has caused his friends' estrangement, as in this scene with his servant, Hernando:

Hernando. ¿Quién será
esta ninfa del Parnaso,
esta infanta del Catay
que los dos recatan tanto?
Don Félix. No sé, y diera por saberlo
cualquier cosa. No he deseado
más en mi vida.

[*Hernando.* I wonder who is / this nymph of Parnassus, / this Princess of Cathay / the two of them care so much about. / *Don Félix.* I don't know, and I would give / anything to know. I have never wanted / anything more in my entire life.]

(3. 2689–94)

Further, Félix insists upon believing that Leonor has rejected him for other men, and he refuses to communicate with her:

Leonor. Aguarda, no vayas
sin oírme.
Don Félix. Ya te he oído.
Leonor. ¿Antes de hablar?
Don Félix. Sí, tirana,
pues antes de hablar, sé ya
que vas a mentir;

[*Leonor.* Wait, don't go / without hearing me. / *Don Félix.* I have heard you already. / *Leonor.* Before I have spoken? / *Don Félix.* Yes, tyrant, / because even before you speak / I know that you are going to lie;]

(1.1090–94)

Ironically, Leonor *does* lie while attempting to persuade Félix of her innocence. In a desperate move, she suggests that the two men who had fought outside her window might have been fighting over another woman in the neighborhood. Don Félix is totally unconvinced by her argument:

piensa otra salida, traza
otra traición, porque ésa

de vecina, amiga, hermana
a quien echarle la culpa
es muy necia y muy usada,
muy frívola, y muy inútil.

[try another way out, scheme / another betrayal, because that one / about a neighbor, a friend, a sister / on whom to put the blame / is very stupid and very worn, / very frivolous and very useless.]
(1.1168–73)

Leonor *is* innocent, but her attempt to win the support of Don Félix fails because he sees through the deception, and because he is fundamentally predisposed to believe in her guilt. These two exchanges illustrate how Calderón's characters interpret situations incorrectly and create ever more serious misunderstandings; they are emblematic of the ways that the "misreading" of intentions (which is actually a manifestation of how a character's horizon of expectations affects his/her actions) can form the basis for the conflict of a comedy.

What occurs at the end of the play is a recognition that order can only be restored when the characters' earlier "readings" are reexamined and "rewritten," that is, when the horizon of expectations that described those characters' initial reactions changes to reflect experience, which can only be acquired through time. This underlines the centuries-old idea that Calderón creates characters who change, who learn how to *obrar bien* [do the right thing] via experience. Consequently, Jauss's intuitions about esthetic reception can and do pertain to the interior levels of *comedia* texts. Just as the reader or spectator reacts to a play based on prior experiences with language, literature, and life, the characters of that play react in complementary fashion. The actualization of those responses is fundamental to the development of the dramatic action and to the resolution of the conflicts offered by the dramatist.

Although the object of this study has not been to analyze the text of Calderón's play in great detail, one key idea does surface: it is imperative to remember that Calderón doesn't merely read his play; he rewrites the ending. He is a reader, but also an active reader, one who converts reception and interpretation into a very specific type of response. In that sense, Calderón writes a new play, one that will later be re-read and re-written by Antonio de Escamilla, the *autor* who compiled the text, by Vera Tassis, who printed it as part of the *Novena parte* in 1691, and by readers and editors of the succeeding centuries.

As we have seen in this analysis, Jauss's ideas on reading and on literary history can serve as metaphors for the relationships between the characters of the play. Changing horizons of expectations are clearly an essential part of the conflict that defines all drama, but they particularly relate to the kinds of conflicts that operate in a play of comic intrigue, such as *Cada uno para sí.* Jauss's theories do not change Calderón's text, but they can change the way we look at it:

> The very history of effects and the interpretation of an event or work of the past enables us to understand it as a plurality of meanings that was not yet perceivable to its contemporaries. ("The Identity" 146–47)

As we search for ways to help us make the *comedia* intelligible, we can discover uses for the new approaches to language and to literary theory—such as the ideas of a critic like Jauss—that have surfaced in the last half of the twentieth century. Jauss gives us one—although certainly not the only—way to see something new in the plays that we read. His work helps us to unite the present with the past and to join authors, texts, and audiences in new paradigmatic relationships, proving that general theoretical ideas can lead us to develop associations far beyond those originally foreseen by the theorists themselves. The theories of a few years ago become the springboards for the theories of the future as critics' horizons of expectations and experience change with time.

8
Conclusions

A major goal of this study has been the presentation of several relatively new ways of looking at classical Hispanic theater, with the analyses of each of the plays suggesting that contemporary literary theory and philosophy can help to uncover meanings that have not surfaced in previous readings of these dramatic texts. Consequently, this book does not presuppose the presentation of one method—or worse, *the* method—of literary analysis. Rather, the analyses found here focus on language in more diverse ways in the hope that each practical application helps us see something that was always a part of the text, but had never before been articulated.

Moreover, the variety of approaches found in this book was intended to permit a sampling of the possibilities that theory gives to literary criticism, as well as to illustrate the importance of seeking theoretical support wisely. What this means is that if we attempt to force a particular theory on a specific text, we may well reap disastrous results. The philosophy that has informed this book is that, with numerous interpretive tools available to scholars and students of literature, judicious selection is an imperative part of the process of assembling and sustaining an argument. Theory is a tool—one of many—available to the critic, and the informed critic and sensitive reader will choose with discretion.

When it comes to the relationship between theory and the theater, the issues have proven complex because of the many factors affecting the entire theatrical semiotic and the multileveled nature of theatrical communication. Theory has, however, a lengthy association with the theater and with theatrical practice. Since the time of Aristotle, theories of the theater have changed the ways we talk about dramatic texts and perform them onstage. Theory, criticism, and practice have, then, been inextricably linked throughout theatrical history; in a very real sense, the modern idea that there can be no practice without theory fuses with the ancient concept that there can be no theory without practice, since practice allows us to discover how theory functions as an interpretive tool. The analyses in this book have tried to underline the fusion of those two concepts, interrogating not just the primary texts, the dramas of the Golden Age, but the horizons and limits of the theories themselves.

In that sense, theory and practice will never go out of style. As Paul de Man writes in *The Resistance to Theory,* "literary theory is not in danger of going under; it cannot help but flourish, and the more it is resisted, the more it flourishes, since the language it speaks is the language of self-resistance" (20). It may be that the days of semiotic readings that offer only flow charts of symbols and letters are waning, and perhaps we have exhausted the possibilities of deconstructive essays that posit only the death of language and of criticism. Still, we have not yet reached the limits of theoretical interpretation, and we cannot return to the days before theory began to influence literary criticism. Theory has guided practice long enough so that the essence of theory will always be a part of what we do when we sit down with a text in order to try to figure out what *it* does. As Stanley Fish rightly observes:

> any account of what now makes up the practice of literary criticism must include theory. . . . The case for theory's inconsequentiality, even if it is persuasive, will not return us to some precritical state, whether it be thought of as a state of innocence or of know-nothing ignorance. ("Consequences" 453, 455)

Theory is with us for the long haul, and its value to the field of literary criticism will be measured, at least in part, by its pragmatic capabilities and promise: the ways that it helps to guide practice by influencing our approaches to the texts that we deal with every day.

Since so much of contemporary theory focuses on language, our analysis has used what characters in dramatic texts say as a starting point for exploring their meaning, incorporating as a primary focus the idea that speech *is* action. In the case of *La dama boba,* we found that on a fundamental level language is what the play was all about, and that characters tended to speak in such a self-referential manner that they created a kind of linguistic superstructure in which words became the objects that motivated the course of the dramatic action. The subversion and support of the conventions governing communication and their concomitant relationship to communities of speakers formed the basis of our discussion of *Entre bobos anda el juego.* In *La verdad sospechosa* and

La dama duende, names—proper and otherwise—also highlighted our appreciation of characterization and our attempts to resolve certain hermeneutical questions. The concept of the self-consciously framed language game served to explicate a number of the dramatic and theatrical transactions of *El caballero de Olmedo.* In *Fuenteovejuna,* written discourse functioned in opposition to speech, which had the effect of heightening the importance of each element (separately and collectively) and of putting into question issues such as truth and justice. Finally, the concept of the esthetics of reception served as a springboard for examining the nature of interpretation in *Cada uno para sí:* the characters' linguistic responses related to the ways they received information and learned to "read" their environment. The ways that words functioned in each of these plays, however, interrelated to a remarkable degree; the dramas of the Golden Age shared a great deal with regard to their creators' perceptions of the relationships existing between language, plot, theme, and characterization. In each chapter, discourse was marked in a very special way as presenting the foregrounding of language, of communication, of social contracts.

What are the results of such linguistically oriented approaches to Golden Age drama? For one thing, we may begin to comprehend more fully the real power of linguistic and theatrical convention in the *comedia.* Linguistic convention, however, is part of the larger picture of how people use language within a linguistic community and includes the far-reaching influence of verbal acts, as well as the consequences of not speaking, of not following the rules, and of straying from the norm. The kinds of verbal games that are played throughout *comedia* texts (including word play, deliberate ambiguity, debating for the sheer love of debating, and willed obfuscation) affect such questions as those dealing with who is (really) in control. We have seen that some characters seem to become dynamic and/or authoritative *because* of language, although others are merely dragged along by its force. Moreover, we have also seen language as one of the few strategies open to Golden Age women who wanted to attain the power and control that were otherwise unavailable to them.

The examination of the relationship between linguistic and theatrical convention also reveals yet another common thread linking a number of these plays: an emphasis on the similarities and differences between written and oral discourse. The conflict between speech and writing and the subsequent overturning of hierarchical relationships emerges as a theme—or at least as a subtheme—of several of the representative texts we have studied. In fact, what a number of *comedia* texts seem to suggest is a view that discourse in general is a subtext, or a pretext, for undercutting and overturning the "obvious," surface level of the play. In that sense, language is a tool for interrogating the status quo, both of the *comedia* and Golden Age society.

Language in the theater always has had a profoundly important role. In these seven plays, discourse is underscored in even more fundamental ways, ways that invite the critic to collude with the text in order to see something else—something that was "*always already* there" (Harari 37), but that resurfaced with the help of some of the theoretical tools available to the critics of today. Language in the *comedia* does influence the reception of the text and a reader's response to it. The union of theory and practice can allow us to explore new readings by linking the present with the past in the fusion of twentieth-century thought and seventeenth-century drama.

Appendix: Plot Summaries

Chapter 1. *La dama boba* [*The Lady Simpleton*], Lope de Vega

The principal characters of *La dama boba* are two sisters, Finea (the simpleton) and Nise (the intelligent sister), who are courted by two suitors, Liseo and Laurencio. The girls' father, Otavio, has decided to give a large dowry to Finea, thinking that no man would agree to marry her without the hope of financial reward. Although both gallants then try to win Finea's hand, Laurencio achieves his goal, since he has made Finea fall in love with him: love functions as the teacher that transforms the simple woman into an intelligent one. Finea's rise is matched by Nise's fall, as the formerly intelligent (although pedantic) sister gradually loses the control she once enjoyed.

Finea's newfound wit leads her to manipulate her father into agreeing to her marriage to Laurencio. She hides Laurencio in the attic and tells her father that Laurencio has gone to Toledo. After Otavio finds Laurencio and threatens to kill him, Finea states that since she had named the attic Toledo, she hadn't lied. The play ends with Finea's betrothal to Laurencio and Nise's to Liseo.

Chapter 2. *Entre bobos anda el juego* [*All the Players Were Fools]*, Francisco de Rojas Zorrilla

This play is called a *comedia de figurón,* a farce whose principal character was presented as a caricature; these comedies were particularly popular in the last half of the seventeenth century. Raymond MacCurdy describes this type of play as follows:

> The *comedia de figurón* is usually defined as a comedy in which the principal character is a supreme eccentric: he is vain, arrogant, presumptuous, crass, and often freakish in appearance. He is, in brief, the very opposite of the handsome, romantic, gallant heroes who abound in the *comedias de capa y espada.* Interestingly, however, the *comedia de figurón* has been singled out as an effective vehicle for social

> criticism, since its burlesque tone affords the dramatist the utmost freedom to satirize Spanish customs and institutions. (*Spanish Drama of the Golden Age* 517)

A major Spanish custom satirized in this comedy is that of arranged marriages. Doña Isabel's father has arranged for her to marry the wealthy but grotesquely undesirable Don Lucas del Cigarral, a man who is stingy in every area except language. Whenever don Lucas talks, he bores his listeners with overblown language and long-winded stories. Don Lucas, however, is not the only character who abuses language. Don Luis, another suitor of Doña Isabel and an equally ridiculous fool, uses an even more affected linguistic style. Don Lucas, anxious to impress his fiancée, asks his young cousin, Don Pedro, to stand in for him, à la Cyrano de Bergerac.

As the comedy progresses, Don Pedro and Doña Isabel fall in love. The two engage in a number of love debates, whose purpose is both to display their linguistic virtuosity and to underline the ancient battle of the sexes. At the end of the play, when the young lovers are finally forced to confess their deception, Don Lucas vows that the two will marry, but that their marriage will be characterized by language. The penniless couple will be forced to use language as food and clothing, since they will have no other way to support themselves.

Chapter 3. *La verdad sospechosa* [*The Suspect Truth*], Juan Ruiz de Alarcón

At the beginning of this play, Don García, the protagonist, returns home to Madrid from Salamanca, where he has been enjoying the wild and carefree life of a student. Don García's father, Don Beltrán, finds out from his son's tutor, the Letrado (graduate or lawyer—a man of letters), that Don García has the reputation of being an inveterate liar. One of the first people Don García sees in Madrid is Doña Jacinta; he instantly falls in love with her. Coincidentally, Don Beltrán has arranged for García to marry Jacinta, hoping to get him married off quickly before society finds out about his lying, but the course of love does not run smooth. Don García has innocently confused the name of the woman he first saw on the street with that of Jacinta's cousin, Lucrecia.

Consequently, thinking that his beloved's name is Lucrecia, Don

García embarks on a series of campaigns to forestall the arranged marriage. He falsely tells his father that he is already married to a Doña Sancha from Salamanca, and he tells other lies to dissuade a competing suitor (Don Juan) from courting Jacinta. The confusion mounts when García courts Jacinta but calls her "Lucrecia"; this makes Jacinta furious and causes the real Lucrecia to fall in love with him. At the end of the play, García's mistaken assumption about Jacinta's name combines with his own lying to produce an ironic ending. Since he has insisted on marrying "Lucrecia," Don García is forced to marry the real Lucrecia, and he loses Jacinta to Don Juan. The play, then, ends with the punishment of the liar: he marries a beautiful and noble woman, but she is not the women he loves. Ironically, in spite of his other examples of lying, in this case, García has not lied, but has merely misindentified Jacinta, a fact that undercuts the moralistic tone of the comedy.

Chapter 4. *El caballero de Olmedo* [*The Knight from Olmedo*], Lope de Vega

El caballero de Olmedo derives from a popular ballad. The play begins like a typical Golden Age love comedy, but it ends tragically. Don Alonso, the knight from Olmedo, has fallen in love with Doña Inés, using a go-between, Fabia, to help win her hand in marriage. Fabia is successful in piquing Doña Inés's interest; they all decide that she and Don Alonso's servant, Tello, will go to Doña Inés's house disguised as a nun and a Latin teacher in order to facilitate the sending of messages between the two lovers. Doña Inés has another suitor, however. Don Rodrigo's jealousy over the love between Alonso and Inés leads him to vow revenge against the knight—even though Don Alonso saves Rodrigo's life.

As the play draws to a close, Don Alonso decides to leave the town of Medina (where Doña Inés lives) to visit his parents in Olmedo. While on the road, he runs into a peasant singing a song that presages Alonso's death; he later meets the Shadow, who warns him to turn back. Alonso bravely continues his journey, but Don Rodrigo and his men fatally ambush the knight. The drama ends when the king, who has heard about Rodrigo's cruel act, orders him put to death.

Chapter 5. *La dama duende* [*]The Spirit Lady*], Pedro Calderón de la Barca

Doña Angela, a young widow, is a virtual prisoner in her own home; her over-protective brothers, Don Juan and Don Luis, try to keep her away from men, but Angela sneaks out of the house to flirt, wearing a cloak that hides her face. The play opens after Angela, having discovered that Luis has joined the crowd of male admirers, runs away while her brother pursues the "mystery woman." Angela asks a stranger to help her escape. This man turns out to be Don Juan's old war buddy, Don Manuel, who has just arrived to visit his friend. Don Manuel intercedes and is slightly wounded by Don Luis.

This comedy is about the clever Doña Angela's machinations to win the hand of Don Manuel. Don Juan installs his friend in a bedroom that contains a cupboard concealing a secret passage; he doesn't tell Manuel about the passage and he believes that his sister doesn't know about it, either. Doña Angela does find out about it, however, and she delights in sneaking into the room when Manuel is away, leaving him gifts and notes signed by the "Spirit Lady" and spiriting him away to a lavish banquet. The comic possibilities of these intrigues are underscored by Manuel's servant, Cosme, who superstitiously believes in the existence of this phantom woman.

At the end of the play, however, the comedy threatens to become a tragedy: Don Luis finds the two lovers together and threatens to kill them. Doña Angela confesses her double identity, Manuel proposes to the woman with whom he has fallen in love, and the play ends happily with the promise of marriage between the two.

Chapter 6. *Fuenteovejuna* [*The Sheep Well*], Lope de Vega

This famous play describes events, recorded in the historical chronicles of the era, that occurred in 1476, during the period when Ferdinand and Isabella were warring with Portugal. Lope's play dramatizes what happens when a town, Fuenteovejuna, rebels against the tyranny of its cruel Commander, the Knight of Calatrava, Fernán Gómez de Guzmán. The Commander has treated the villagers with arrogant disdain, has seduced or raped the local women, and has given counsel and support to another

Knight of Calatrava (a military order that was supporting the King of Portugal), the young Rodrigo Téllez Girón, in his siege of Cuidad Real. The drama's two plots, the military-Cuidad Real plot and the local oppression-Fuenteovejuna plot, are united by the figure of the Commander.

In the town of Fuenteovejuna, we witness how the Commander's cruel acts increasingly disturb the harmony of the villagers' lives. The Commander interrupts Laurencia and Frondoso's wedding, ordering that Frondoso will be killed, carrying Laurencia off to his quarters so that he can ravish her, and breaking the staff of office over the head of Esteban, the mayor and Laurencia's father. These acts provoke the villagers to violence: the entire village—both men and women—acts as a unit to kill the Commander, although they continue to proclaim their loyalty to the king and queen. The villagers of Fuenteovejuna also expect communal punishment, and the Catholic monarchs (Ferdinand and Isabella) do send a royal investigator to ascertain the truth about what happened; the monarchs seek to protect the social hierarchy and punish anarchy. The investigator tortures the entire town, but every one of the villagers answers his question, "Who killed the Commander?," with "Fuenteovejuna did it." The villagers thus accept communal responsibility for the murder, and King Ferdinand, faced with the choice of killing or pardoning the entire town, uses the excuse that without written confirmation of the correct murderer's identity, he will pardon them all.

This pardon has been presaged by the king's pardon of the young Rodrigo Téllez Girón, who had acted imprudently in siding with Portugal and who had treated Ciudad Real cruelly. The violence of the early acts of the play has been replaced by the restoration of order and peace.

Chapter 7. *Cada uno para sí* [*Every Man for Himself*], Pedro Calderón de la Barca

This complicated play consists of a number of love triangles, the result of having three men and two women vie for each other's love. Misunderstandings and unrequited love fuse to create a complex tissue of confusion, passion, and assaulted honor. Don Félix, fearing that two other men have been courting Leonor behind his back, unjustly accuses her of infidelity. He later becomes even more upset when he learns that those two men are his friends, Carlos and Enrique. Carlos and Enrique also become angry with each when they think (incorrectly) that they are both rivals for Leonor's hand, but the issue is further complicated when Enrique learns that he has to investigate Carlos because of a prior obligation (involving Carlos's investiture into the Knights of Santiago). He cannot duel with him until the investigation is completed. Leonor's cousin, Violante, reacts strongly when she hears that her lover, Carlos, has been unfaithful: she refuses to marry him, becomes infatuated with Félix, and is unhappy with the idea that Félix would rather be with Leonor.

All of these interwoven triangles threaten to explode in violence. While Enrique and Carlos are engaged in a duel, Félix arrives to stop his friends from killing themselves. He discovers, however, that the woman they are fighting over is his own Leonor, so he joins the duel to fight against them both. The triple duel scene is interrupted by the women and their fathers, who straighten out the mess and marry the original couples to each other. The innocent Leonor marries Félix, the man she loves and deserves, the flighty Violante marries her original suitor, Carlos (although the two don't really love each other and although each has been unfaithful to the other), and Enrique is left without a bride.

From the drama's title on, what Calderón dramatizes and criticizes in this play is the idea that every man (or woman) acts for himself (or herself). When something seems to stand in the way of achieving true love (or money and social position, which is what occurs in the subplots involving the servants and the women's fathers), the bonds of friendship or family ties fly out the window.

Notes

Introduction: Language and the *Comedia*

1. In Bruce W. Wardropper's description of the effects of poststructuralist criticism on Hispanic scholarship, he observes, "in recent years the literary avant-garde has been long on theory and short on actual criticism" ("An Apology for Philology" 177). This would suggest that many of the people who are working with theory do not convert their discoveries into practice; interpretation is clearly affected as a result. As for the *comedia* and its scholars, the comments that James A. Parr made in 1974 are, unfortunately, still viable:

> we are, in the majority, at some distance from the mainstream of modern critical theory and practice. . . . What we need, in any case, is not a special approach stressing the peculiar nature of the *comedia* but simply the application of existing and widely accepted critical insights and procedures. ("An Essay on Critical Method" 434, 439)

2. See Richard Levin's *New Readings vs. Old Plays: Recent Trends in the Reinterpretation of English Renaissance Drama.*

3. See Jauss's work on the nature of the horizons of expectations and experience, as well as my discussion of the topic in chapter 7.

4. Elam notes, "the written text is as much a permutation of the text of the performance as it is in turn permuted by that text. The inter-textual relationship here is unusually privileged, since the written text, in its permuted form . . . is always a factor contributory to the performance text" ("Language in the Theater" 158).

5. See Elam ("Language in the Theater," *Semiotics*), Elizabeth Burns *(Theatricality),* and Deirdre Burton (*Dialogue and Discourse,* "Conversation Pieces") for more detailed descriptions of the multileveled quality of discourse in theatrical texts; further, see Mary Louise Pratt (*Toward a Speech Act Theory,* "Ideology") for her illuminating comments on the application of speech-act theory to literary discourse.

6. Elam notes that "'Gesture,' indeed, is essentially a rhetorical mode of action. Action becomes gesture when it assumes a semiotic function" ("Language in the Theater" 146).

7. Elam observes that poetic language in the theater makes "conspicuous"

> the *written text,* as a composed artifact produced by a poet. Elaborate uses of language on stage, therefore, signify an allegiance to the literary, to a premeditated compositional act which to some extent "determines" what transpires on stage. Poetic dialogue, in brief, connotes authorship. ("Language in the Theater" 152)

8. I have used the following editions of the dramas analyzed in this book:

Vega Carpio, Lope de. *La dama boba.* Edited by Diego Marín. 5th ed. Madrid: Cátedra, 1981.

Rojas Zorrilla, Francisco de. *Entre bobos anda el juego.* In *Spanish Drama of the*

Golden Age, ed. Raymond MacCurdy, 521–72. New York: Appleton-Century-Crofts, 1971.
Ruiz de Alarcón, Juan. *La verdad sospechosa.* In *Diez Comedias del Siglo de Oro,* edited by José Martel and Hymen Alpern. 2d. ed., 517–604. New York: Harper and Row, 1968.
Vega Carpio, Lope de. *El caballero de Olmedo.* Edited by Francisco Rico. 6th ed. Madrid: Cátedra, 1985.
Calderón de la Barca, Pedro. *La dama duende.* Edited by Angel Valbuena Briones. 6th ed. Madrid: Cátedra, 1984.
Vega Carpio, Lope de. *Fuente Ovejuna.* Edited by Juan María Marín. 8th ed. Madrid: Cátedra, 1987.
Calderón de la Barca, Pedro. *Cada uno para sí.* Edited by José Ruano de la Haza. Kassel: Reichenberger, 1982.
All act, scene (when so used by the editors), and verse numbers will be indicated within the text of each chapter.

Chapter 1. Language as Subject and Object of Lope's *La dama boba*

1. See Walter Cohen's *Drama of a Nation: Public Theater in Renaissance England and Spain* and John Loftis's *The Spanish Plays of Neoclassical England* for detailed examinations of the links between Spain and England during the sixteenth and seventeenth centuries. Cohen observes:

> Spanish and English plays stand apart from all other European drama because they synthesize native popular and neoclassical learned traditions. Although the two theaters developed in relative isolation from each other, they form a group because both combined what elsewhere appeared only separately. (17)

Certainly, Cohen approaches the similarities between Spanish and English Renaissance theater from an ideological rather than a linguistic perspective, although he does introduce such linguistic issues as theatrical self-consciousness, asides, proverbs, and wordplay (178). Most importantly, however, by examining the historical, political, and social institutions that surrounded the development of the public theater, he helps to contextualize the two countries' climates of artistic creation and production.

2. Some poststructuralist critics, however, have criticized speech act theory as being essentially incompatible with their own ideas on the indeterminacy of language, on the distinction between speech and writing, etc. The debate between John R. Searle and Jacques Derrida, pitting Austin and speech act theory against Derridean deconstruction, was carried out on the pages of *Glyph* in 1977. As other critics joined the debate, it spilled over onto the pages of *Diacritics* (Gayatri Spivak's "Revolutions That as Yet Have No Model," 1980), *Centrum* (Mary Louise Pratt's "The Ideology of Speech Act Theory," 1981), *Critical Inquiry* (Stanley Fish's "With the Compliments of the Author: Reflections on Austin and Derrida," 1982), and even the *New York Review of Books* (Searle's "The Word Turned Upside Down," 1983), among others. It is obvious that these two theoretical approaches have provoked a great deal of discussion in the academic community; the debate is representative of the continuing reexamination of Austin and of the differing views of language that have marked the theoretical scene of the past twenty years.

3. The *gracioso* in the Golden Age was typically the servant who provided comic relief for the play. *Sayagués* was a dialect often used for comic effect. See studies by Angel Valbuena-Briones ("Los papeles cómicos y las hablas dialectales en dos comedias de Calderón"), A. E. Sloman ("The Phonology of Moorish Jargon in Two Works of Early Spanish Dramatists and Lope de Vega"), and John Lihani ("A Literary Jargon of Early Spanish Drama: The Sayagués Dialect"), for analyses of the role of dialect in Hispanic drama.

4. In *How to Do Things with Words*, Austin noted a distinction between literary discourse and ordinary language, labeling the former *parasitic:* "a performative utterance will, for example, be *in a peculiar way* hollow or void if said by an actor on the stage, or if introduced in a poem, or spoken in soliloquy" (22). Subsequent discussions of this issue have interrogated the problems that Austin's statement poses for literary analysis. Along with the majority of Austin's followers, however, I believe that although dramatic discourse is not a completely realistic rendering of everyday conversation (it doesn't contain, for example, the same number of pauses or conversational "fillers"), the types of social contracts formed between speakers and the basic ways that things are done with words are essentially the same in dramatic dialogue as they are in real life.

5. Issues involving power and authority include and relate to Austin's emphasis on the performative notion, "Our word is our bond" (*How to Do* 10), to vocabulary choice, and to forms of address. In addition to these points, however, a whole range of linguistic elements can either support or undercut authority: wordplay, double entendres, ironic or parodic language, verbal duels, half-truths, and deception with the truth *[engañar con la verdad].*

6. See Myra Gann's speech act study of the relationship between the honor code and language in *A secreto agravio, secreta venganza [To Secret Grievance, Secret Revenge]* and Margaret R. Hick's analysis of a similar theme in Lope's *La batalla de honor [The Battle of Honor].*

7. Speech act theorists and other linguists have long debated whether or not language is rule-governed or bound by convention; the debate remains unresolved. See especially Michael Hancher ("Beyond a Speech-Act Theory of Literary Discourse"), H. Paul Grice ("Logic and Conversation"), Mary Louise Pratt *(Toward a Speech Act Theory of Literary Discourse)*, and John R. Searle (*Speech Acts: An Essay in the Philosophy of Langauge* and *Expression and Meaning: Studies in the Theory of Speech Acts*).

8. For the fundamental explanation of language as action, see Austin's discussion of the performative in *How to Do Things with Words* and Felman's application of this concept to Molière's *Don Juan* in *The Literary Speech Act.*

9. See especially studies by Donald R. Larson ("*La dama boba* and the Comic Sense of Life"), Robert ter Horst ("The True Mind of Marriage: Ironies of the Intellect in Lope's *La dama boba*"), James E. Holloway ("Lope's Neoplatonism: *La dama boba*"), and Ronald E. Surtz ("Daughter of Night, Daughter of Light: The Imagery of Finea's Transformation in *La dama boba*") for solid close readings of the play.

10. Richard Hornby's study of the nature of self-conscious language in the theater, *Drama, Metadrama, and Perception,* is a useful analysis of the phenomenon, in that it relates the complex use of metalanguage (and metadiscourse) to the entire notion of self-conscious theater. See also Elam (*Shakespeare's Universe* 19–20).

11. See Elam's introduction to *Shakespeare's Universe of Discourse* for a detailed explanation of the importance of embedded texts (24–32).

12. For a more detailed exploration of the notion of felicity in speech acts, see J. L. Austin *(How to Do Things with Words),* Mary Louise Pratt *(Toward a Speech Act Theory of Literary Discourse),* Shoshana Felman *(The Literary Speech Act),* and Stanley Fish ("How to Do Things with Austin and Searle: Speech-Act Theory and Literary Criticism").

13. In the *comedia,* love and language are inextricably linked. In its highest form, love (as opposed to sexual passion) finds its expression in language, yet it is also language's greatest test, since the dramatist must try to find a means of expressing the unexpressable.

Chapter 2. Grice's Maxims and Rojas Zorrilla's *Entre bobos anda el juego*

1. Although I have tried to use gender-neutral pronouns throughout my analysis, I follow Grice here.

2. See Edward Bullough's "'Psychical Distance' and a Factor in Art and an Esthetic Principle" for an explanation of esthetic distance and the relationship between works of art (particularly in the theater), overdistancing, and underdistancing. As members of an audience, our experience is curiously paradoxical. Often when we note the deliberate noncommunication occurring onstage, we are distanced from the work by a feeling of superiority to the victims of those characters who manipulate language to suit their own purposes; at other times, we identify with the victim or with the clever perpetrator and thus are drawn closer to him or her. This identification creates a close link between characters and audiences. Either way, though, an audience's recognition of the effectiveness of communication onstage—its analysis of who wins and who loses, who dominates and who does not, and who is the victim and who the victimizer—relates directly to the larger communicative exchange, that between an author, a (play) text, and an audience. Consequently, the lack of effective communication onstage leads to a type of communication of a different tenor. The interplay of these multiple levels of communication within the literary-dramatic speech situation provides an opportunity to explore the interweaving of linguistic play and humor in the comedy.

3. See Geoffrey Leech, *Principles of Pragmatics,* especially page 5, for a discussion of the lack of moral constraints associated with these principles.

4. This linking of language, plot, and characterization is, of course, central to the dramatist's creation of meaning. In that sense, I view speech act theory much as does Stanley Fish:

> the ideology of speech act theory is meaning, the assumption of sense and of the possibility of its transmission. . . . Speech act theory is an account of the conditions of intelligibility, of what it means to mean in a community, of the procedures which must be instituted before one can even be said to be understood ("How to Do Things" 243–35).

5. Edwin B. Place offers a clear definition of the *figurón* and of Don Lucas's role in this comedy in "Notes on the Grotesque: The *comedia de figurón* at Home and Abroad." See also Ruiz Ramón's *Historia del teatro español [History of Spanish Theater]* for a comparison between Don Lucas and Don Luis.

6. Keir Elam observes that the embedded text (an "internal 'textual' event—the reading of a poem, say, or of a letter—placed in a 'boxed' position within the

main text and the main performance") illustrates how "dramatic discourse achieves rhetorical or semiotic complexity" (*Semiotics* 24–25).

7. In that context, Raymond MacCurdy notes that characters like Don Lucas in the *comedia de figurón* are radical opposites of the *galanes* [leading male characters] of the *comedia de capa y espada* (517).

8. For a more detailed discussion of appropriateness (felicity) conditions, see Pratt (*Theory* 81–91).

9. See Elam (*Semiotics* and *Shakespeare*) and Hornby *(Drama, Metadrama, and Perception)* on self-conscious language in the theater.

10. The seminal study of the notion of poetic justice in the *comedia* is A. A. Parker's "The Approach to the Spanish Drama of the Golden Age." Parker observes:

> Spanish dramatic plots are constructed on the principle of poetic justice. . . . Poetic justice is a principle of literature and not a fact of experience. In real life evil men may prosper and virtuous men may suffer. But in literature it was, in seventeenth-century Spain, considered fitting that wrongdoing should not go unpunished and that virtue should not remain unrewarded. (7)

11. It should be added that this exploration of the function of language within communities of speakers clearly relates to another oral tradition within society: the popular saying or proverb. The title of Rojas's play is part of a longer saying: "Entre bobos anda el juego, y eran todos fulleros" [All the players were fools, and cardsharps too] (see Maldonado and Correas). In his edition of the play (in *Spanish Drama of the Golden Age*), Raymond MacCurdy observes that the Spanish Royal Academy Dictionary defines the phrase as a " 'frase irónica de que se usa cuando los que tratan alguna cosa son igualmente diestros y astutos.' The title has been translated both as *Merry Sport with Fools* and *Folly Reigns Here*" (note 1, p. 521). A literal translation of the title, *including* the allusion to cardsharps, however, seems even more appropriate. The idea that some players in the game of love cheat is clearly an important aspect of *Entre bobos anda el juego*. Even more interesting is the relationship between this social "maxim" and our discussion of Grice's maxims. In both cases, the ties between discourse and a community of speakers are made explicit: our physical, ethical, and verbal conduct is governed by the communities in which we live and speak.

Chapter 3. Labels and Lies: Names and Don García's World in *La verdad sospechosa*

1. See studies by Walter Poesse *(Juan Ruiz de Alarcón)*, Antonio Castro Leal *(Juan Ruiz de Alarcón: su vida y su obra)*, Louise Fothergill-Payne ("La justicia poética de *La verdad sospechosa*"), Alan Soons ("*La verdad sospechosa* in its Epoch"), Leonard M. DiLillo ("Moral Purpose in Ruiz de Alarcón's *La verdad sospechosa*"), John G. Morton ("Alarcón's *La verdad sospechosa*: Meaning and Didacticism"), James C. Parr ("Honor-Virtue in *La verdad sospechosa* and *Las paredes oyen*"), Robert Fiore ("The Interaction of Motives and Mores in *La verdad sosopechosa*"), and David Darst ("Hidden Truths and Wrong Assumptions in *La verdad sospechosa*"). Special note must be given to those by E. C. Riley ("Alarcón's *mentiroso* in the Light of the Contemporary Theory of Character"), Geoffrey Ribbans ("Lying in the Structure of *La verdad sospechosa*"), and Alan K. Paterson ("Reversal

and Multiple Role-Playing in Alarcón's *La verdad sospechosa*) for their overall comprehensiveness and for their particular relevance to this chapter.

2. Two lucid analyses of the role of discourse in *Le Menteur* are those of John D. Lyons ("Discourse and Authority in *Le Menteur*") and Milorad Margitic ("Le discours direct comme forme verbale d'illusion théâtrale chez Corneille").

3. This view has been supported by Paterson, Soons, Castro Leal, and Poesse.

4. In his chapter on *Richard II* in *The Drama of Speech Acts,* Joseph Porter includes both of these types under the general category of "names." He characterizes both metaphoric (generic) and proper names as equations in which "X is Y" (23–25). In *Expression and Meaning,* John R. Searle describes the variety of linguistic/syntactical devices speakers use to achieve reference with regard to objects (including, of course, people): "whenever a speaker refers he must have some linguistic representation of the object—a proper name, a definite description, etc.—and this representation will represent the object referred to under some *aspect* or other" (142). Saul Kripke uses the term "designator" to cover both names and descriptions. He states, "A description may be used as synonymous with a designator, or it may be used to fix its reference" (*Naming and Necessity* 59). Nothwithstanding the number of distinct theories on naming and reference (including work by such scholars as Frege, Mill, Russell, and Donnellan), in this study I maintain that there exists a fundamental link between the two types of baptisms represented in *La verdad sospechosa* by generic and proper names and by descriptions and identity designators.

5. "Counts as" is a term used in speech act theory to define, in a broad sense, conventions. See, for example, Kent Bach and Robert M. Harnish: "The idea of conventionality is quite broad; our conception of convention captures, and is meant to capture, but one part of it. For us conventions are *counts-as* rules and nothing else" (*Linguistic Communiction and Speech Acts* 108). I have used "counts as" in this section of my analysis because it is a logical, understandable expression of generic naming.

6. See Castro Leal: "Las mentiras de don García son un triunfo de la imaginación sobre la realidad y constituyen una verdadera rebelión poética" [Don García's lies are a triumph of imagination over reality, and they constitute a veritable poetic rebellion] (*Juan Ruiz de Alarcón: su vida y su obra* 36).

7. E. C. Riley observes that García "habitually assumes a role that flatters his vanity—wealthy nabob, lavish host, successful gallant, deadly adversary in a duel" ("Alarcón's *mentiroso*" 226). Alan Soons notes, "He presents himself, to each of the other characters, as a 'metaphor'—García as something else—and it is through the plausibility of these presentations that he remains master of the action of the play" ("*La verdad sospechosa* in its Epoch" 242).

8. In his analysis of the levels of discourse in Corneille's *Le Menteur,* Lyons describes how Dorante differs from Alcippe and Géronte with regard to their view of nobility:

> For [Géronte and Alcippe] a noble is expected to establish his authority by *doing,* not merely by saying. For Géronte, as for Alcippe, no amount of *esprit* can compensate for a lack of courage and, as a corollary, the past and memory have particular importance. . . . This system of authority, which is that of the feudal aristocracy, does not accept the disruption of time and space so characteristic of the man à la mode. ("Discourse and Authority in *Le Menteur*" 160–61)

9. Paterson views the duel as a "real show-stopper." He observes that "García has to put to ridicule one of the traditional rituals enacted in the name of worth,

namely the ultimate defence of one's name by seeking satisfaction in the challenge and the duel" ("Reversal and Multiple Role-Playing" 365).

10. See Austin's *How to Do Things with Words* for its discussion of the performative notion that our word is our bond. Pratt's "The Ideology of Speech Act Theory" delineates the current direction of sociolinguistic research and details subsequent work in the field, in which her own research (1977 and 1980) has had a major impact.

11. Ribbans discusses lying in *La verdad sospechosa* on both the individual level and from a societal context. He notes that in the *indiano* lie, García "has taken on more than he can manage," and he links the action of the play to "García's self-confident imprudence" ("Lying in the Structure" 198).

12. Paterson notes that "the outstanding formal features of reversal and the protagonist's multiple role-playing in *La verdad sospechosa* are complementary aspects of a fundamental and rigorous social critique" ("Reversal and Multiple Role-Playing" 366–67).

13. See Elias Rivers's analysis of *La Estrella de Sevilla* for a related examination of the relationship between speech and writing in the *comedia*.

Chapter 4. Language Games in the Theater: The Case of *El caballero de Olmedo*

1. Wittgenstein, who died in 1951, left a relatively brief, but influential, legacy in his observations on the nature of language. Only two of his books were published during his lifetime. The most famous, his *Philosophical Investigations,* which is representative of the last stage of his philosophical writings, first appeared two years after his death. Wittgenstein's concept of the language game was first proposed in the *Brown Book* (1933–35; published in 1958), a collection of notes that, along with the *Blue Book,* formed the *Preliminary Studies* for the *Philosophical Investigations* (1941–48; published in 1953). In the *Philosophical Investigations,* Wittgenstein explored the relationship between philosophy and the ambiguities of linguistic expression, stressing that philosophers need to concern themselves with studying the proper use of language. This approach, known as ordinary language philosophy, has as one of its key elements Wittgenstein's notion of the language game.

Wittgenstein himself never fully defined the language game, although he referred to it countless times in the series of questions and suppositions that comprise the *Philosophical Investigations:*

> Here we come up against the great question that lies behind all these considerations. For someone might object against me: "You take the easy way out! You talk about all sorts of language-games, but have nowhere said what the essence of a language-game, and hence of language is: what is common to all these activities, and what makes them into language or parts of language." (*PI* I, Section 65)

Henry Staten ("Wittgenstein's Boundaries") helps to clarify what Wittgenstein meant by the term "language game":

> the concept of a game is the one that he uses to understand language itself, in the analogy or metaphor or catachresis of the "language-game." It is of *language-games,* the main subject of his investigations, that he wants above all to avoid giving general definitions. In remark 71 Wittgenstein tells how one explains what a game is: one gives

examples, not so that the learner should find in them the common factor *(das Gemeinsame)*, but rather so that he should learn how to *use* these examples. (312)

The lack of concrete definitions in Wittgenstein's theories does not mean to suggest that his ideas are so general as to be unusable in interpretive practice. Nonetheless, Austin E. Quigley ("Wittgenstein's Philosophizing and Literary Theorizing") observes:

> Wittgenstein offers us no distinctions, and (apart from a sprinkling of characteristic metaphors) no highly developed technical vocabulary. While a Freudian analysis of a literary text instantly declares itself to be so, it can be difficult to identify as such a Wittgensteinian analysis. There is no elaborate jargon to give the game away, no set of presuppositions to be posited and illustrated, no characteristic goals that pronounce themselves in advance. (210–11)

Although Quigley's comments suggest that Wittgenstein offers an unaccommodating tool for literary analysis, I would maintain that Keir Elam's successful application of the language game to drama in *Shakespeare's Universe of Discourse* displays a comprehensive and comprehensible union of theory and practice.

2. Elam differentiates *metalanguage* from *metadiscourse:*

> Language used to comment directly on language itself is generally known as *metalanguage* . . . "meta" having here the Greek sense of a secondary or parasitic "going beyond." And by analogy, a use of language which in turn frames, or "goes beyond", language *in use* can be termed *metadiscourse.* The extraordinary metadiscursive density of Shakespeare's comedies is one of the chief sources of their formidable rhetorical complexity and formal self-awareness. (*Shakespeare's Universe* 19)

3. The Celestina was the go-between (who was also associated with witchcraft) who facilitated the meetings between the two lovers of Fernando de Rojas's *La Celestina* (1499), namely Calisto and Melibea. In this early tragicomedy, Calisto proclaims his love in a famous lament, saying that he adores Melibea and, more significantly, that he has *become* Melibea. This speech, undoubtedly well-known to Golden Age audiences, is reprised in Lope's *El caballero de Olmedo,* offering an intertextual echo that reveals the doubling of the original. Fabia is also clearly a character that Golden Age audiences would recognize. She is obviously a doubling of the Celestina, but Lope reinforces the point with direct allusions to her literary ancestor.

4. See studies by Alan Soons ("Towards an Interpretation of *El caballero de Olmedo*") and A. S. Gérard ("Baroque Unity and the Dualities of *El caballero de Olmedo*") for a discussion of the role of clothing imagery in the play. Other key studies of imagery, symbolism, and metaphor in *El caballero de Olmedo* include those of McCrary, Hesse, King, Sage, Wardropper, Casa, and Turner.

5. Embedded texts illustrate a mode of recursion typical of the framed game: "dramatic discourse achieves rhetorical or semiotic complexity through the embedding of different kinds of discursive and textual units: games nesting in other (framing) games in a potentially infinite regressive series" (Elam, *Shakespeare's Universe* 24).

6. See especially studies by Américo Castro *("El caballero de Olmedo")* and Bruce Wardropper ("The Criticism of the Spanish *Comedia: El Caballero de Olmedo*") for an examination of the importance of physical movement in the play.

7. This early warning is echoed in Act 3 by the *Labrador*'s words to Don

Alonso ("Volved, volved a Medina," ["Go back, go back to Medina"] 3.2412) and his song:

> Sombras le avisaron
> que no saliese,
> y le aconsejaron
> que no se fuese
> el caballero,
> la gala de Medina,
> la flor de Olmedo.

> [Shadows warned him / against going / and they advised him / not to leave: / that knight, / Medina's handsomest, / Olmedo's flower.]
>
> (3.2386–92)

The play thus comes full circle: Don Alonso refuses to heed both the warnings of Inés, disguised as a *labradora*, and those of the *labrador*, and he ends up paying with his life.

Chapter 5. *La dama duende* and the Shifting Characterization of Calderón's Diabolical Angel

1. For a more detailed discussion of the androcentric oppositions that dominate in literary texts, see K. K. Ruthven's *Feminist Literary Studies* (40–42) and Toril Moi's *Sexual/Textual Politics* (102–26).

2. Adrienne Schizzano Mandel's unique analysis of the linguistic structure of *La dama duende* underlines a central point of this reading: "El lenguaje parece actuar a modo de disfraz que encubre y descubre una realidad" [Language seems to act as a disguise that conceals and reveals a reality] (42).

3. In *The Limits of Illusion*, Anthony Cascardi describes *La dama duende* as a "dialectic of positive and negative, inside and out, male and female, of reversible roles and values" (27). Notwithstanding Cascardi's exuberant imagery ("Calderón's phantom lady flits across the stage like a bundle of veiled motion, a volatile packet of erotic energy, chameleon-like in her *duende*-like nature" [25]; "Like any shield . . . the house and its walls are vulnerable to penetration. . . . The house of males is itself a threat to Angela's honor, but it is Angela who penetrates the partition between her room and Manuel's," [28–29]), his insightful study complements the exploration of Angela as angel and demon that informs this chapter. It should be noted, however, that discussions (including my own) that emphasize binary oppositions also reinforce—at least to a certain degree—traditional patriarchal models of separation and disunion.

4. Richard Hornby's lucid study of metadrama *(Drama, Metadrama, and Perception)* describes role-playing within the role as being particularly effective for exploring role and character:

> Role playing within the role sets up a special acting situation that goes beyond the usual exploration of specific roles; it exposes the very nature of role itself. (72)

Hornby's analysis is particularly relevant to the case of *La dama duende,* because it underscores the dualistic nature of Doña Angela's characterization:

> Among other things, role playing within the role is an excellent means of delineating character, by showing not only who the character is, but what he wants to be. When a

playwright depicts a character who is himself playing a role, there is often the suggestion that, ironically, the role is closer to the character's true self than his everyday, "real" personality. (67)

5. See Merry Weisner's examination of women in the sixteenth and seventeenth centuries ("Women's Defense of Their Public Role") for a discussion of the increasing restrictions that widows faced in the Golden Age. Further, see Honig's analysis of the implications of such cultural realities in *La dama duende.*

6. See de Armas (*The Invisible Mistress* 46) for an analysis of the implications of Eve, the Tree of Knowledge, and curiosity in the creation of the Invisible Mistress plot of which *La dama duende* is representative.

7. In *The Development of Imagery in Calderón's Comedias,* William R. Blue succinctly analyzes the problems that other characters encounter in pinning down Angela's identity. See especially 44–47.

8. Calderón includes Angela as part of an image of heaven and hell in act 2:

Don Manuel. Imagen es
de la más rara beldad,
que el soberano pincel
ha obrado.
Cosme. Así es verdad;
porque sólo ha hizo él.
Don Manuel. Más que la luz resplandecen
sus ojos.
Cosme. Lo cierto es,
que son sus ojos luceros
del cielo de Lucifer.
Don Manuel. Cada cabello es un rayo
del sol.
Cosme. Hurtáronlos de él.
Don Manuel. Una estrella es cada rizo.
Cosme. Sí será; porque también
se las trujeron acá,
o una parte de las tres.

[*Don Manuel:* She's the image of the rarest beauty that the hand of God has ever drawn. *Cosme:* That's true; because He alone did such a thing. *Don Manuel:* Her eyes shine brighter than light. *Cosme:* True—her eyes are like Lucifer's lamps fallen from heaven. *Don Manuel:* Each hair shines like the rays of the sun. *Cosme:* He must have stolen them from heaven. *Don Manuel:* Her curls are like stars. *Cosme:* Of course, because they're also brought from there—or from Heaven, Purgatory, or Hell.]

(2.2041–54)

9. See Sandra Gilbert and Susan Gubar's *The Madwoman in the Attic.* In Nina Auerbach's *Woman and the Demon,* a study complementing that of Gilbert and Gubar, Auerbach states:

It may not be surprising that female demons bear an eerie resemblance to their angelic counterparts, though characteristics that are suggestively implicit in the angel come to the fore in the demon. Their covert identification is motivated by their common cause: both are illicit invaders of traditional Anglican symbolism, announcing a new dispensation that is of pre-Christian antiquity. In the Socratic usage in the OED, "demon" need not designate an evil spirit alone but may incorporate divinity into its supernatural power: "[thing] of divine or demonic nature or character." The Soothsayer in Shakespeare's *Antony and Cleopatra* uses "demon" interchangeably with "angel": "Thy demon, that's thy spirit which keeps thee, is / Noble, courageous, high, unmatchable, / Where Caesar's is not. But near him, thy angel / Becomes afeard" (II, iii, 18–21). (75)

Auerbach's union of the angel and the demon, studied from the perspective of Victorian myth and complementing Gilbert and Gubar's analysis, is especially resonant of the union of these two elements in *La dama duende.*

10. Honig discusses the nature of Doña Angela's female role in courtship: "Her incursions into his apartment and his later induction into hers are all carried out . . . to test his fitness for the role she has chosen for him. If he is a true gentleman, and really prizes the mystery of courtship, he will be worthy of her love" (*Calderón and the Seizures of Honor* 133–34). Angel Valbuena Briones underscores the social and cultural implications of Angela's actions when he observes, "La lucha vital, pero ingeniosa, de doña Angela en contra de las convenciones sociales para obtener el marido que anhela manifiesta una causa con la que las damas de la época se identificaron fácilmente" [Doña Angela's vital, but ingenious struggle against social conventions to get the husband she wants illustrates a cause with which the women of the epoch could readily identify] ("Los papeles cómicos" 41).

11. In *Calderón: The Secular Plays,* ter Horst explains the intertextual nature of Calderón's references to the romances of chivalry and, specifically, to *Don Quixote* (see especially 73–74).

12. This apparent ambiguity in Calderón's presentation of Doña Angela may be explained by the relationship between society and women in the seventeenth century: "If a society demands that its women both are and are not angelic, then its representations of them will be ambivalent" (Ruthven, *Feminist Literary Studies* 75). Frederick de Armas interestingly uses similar words to describe this "basic ambiguity, this ambivalence in man's view of woman. . . . This essential ambiguity in the portrayal of women will become particularly striking in Golden Age versions of the Invisible Mistress plot" (*The Invisible Mistress* 17).

13. See Adrienne Rich, "Planetarium," *Poems, Selected and New, 1950–74.*

Chapter 6. "Violent Hierarchies": The Deconstructive Voice and Writing Undone in *Fuenteovejuna*

1. J. Hillis Miller observes that "Any reading can be shown to be a misreading on evidence drawn from the text itself" ("Stevens' Rock" 333).

2. Douglas Atkins describes the situation:

> To attempt merely to replace one term in a hierarchy with another is to remain within hierarchical and oppositional (that is, metaphysical, logocentric) thinking. What distinguishes deconstruction from what may be called de-struction is precisely that the movement or play does not stop with an initial reversal . . . the newly elevated term is reinscribed in the field of language and shown to oscillate ceaselessly with its apparent opposite. (*Reading Deconstruction* 84–85)

3. Several critics have suggested other sources for Lope's play. Duncan Moir notes the importance of Covarrubias's *Emblemas morales,* Claude Aníbal suggests the primary source as Palencia's *Crónica de Enrique IV,* and Rafael Ramírez Arellano uses documents from Córdoba to support his claim that the villagers' revolt was motivated by events that occurred in that city.

4. Manuel Durán notes that Lope's theater was "un teatro en que el pasado y

el presente se unían, se compenetraban, se explicaban mutuamente" [a theater in which the present and past came together, interpenetrated, and mutually explained each other] ("Lope y el teatro" 4).

5. Leo Spitzer observes that "Lope worked as it were, from the historical battle-cries, backward to their metaphysical force" ("A Central Theme" 290). William McCrary notes, "it indicates that the dramatist has interpreted known facts in the light of a preconceived metaphysical system" ("*Fuenteovejuna*" 180).

6. The *Chronica,* for example, describes the villagers' violent acts toward the Comendador: they threw his body out the window and onto their waiting swords and lances *although he was still alive* [my emphasis], they broke his teeth, and refused to return the Comendador's body to his servants for burial (79).

7. Consequently, modern interpretations that view *Fuenteovejuna* as the archetypical drama of revolution, evidenced by the popularity of the play in post-Revolutionary Russia, have ignored what many critics have seen as the dramatist's clear support for the feudal system that existed in the town. These critics maintain that *Fuenteovejuna* is not about the rebellion of the masses against the system in which they lived, but about their rebellion against one abusive Comendador. Bruce Wardropper explains:

> The people of Fuente Ovejuna do not revolt to change the social organization, but merely to remove an unjust office-holder within the existing social structure. They rise up against Fernán Gómez, the man; not against the system of *encomienda* under which they live. In destroying the man, they incidentally destroy the system, but only because the social reform happens to be a paternalistic sovereign's will. ("*Fuente Ovejuna*" 168–69)

8. See Duncan Moir:

> It is necessary, in the drama of the Golden Age, to avoid an ending which could suggest condonement of rebellion against established authority, and the chronicle tale provides just the sort of conclusion which can be both acceptable to the stage censors and dramatically satisfactory, but, even at the end of *Fuenteovejuna,* we still *feel* that the villagers' killing Fernán Gómez de Guzmán is justified and we are pleased by it, even though we may *reason* that they ought to have . . . gone to Ferdinand and Isabel to seek justice, instead of killing the Comendador themselves. ("Lope de Vega's *Fuenteovejuna*" 541)

9. For a discussion of the interplay between the written and oral traditions in the Golden Age, see Elias Rivers's *Quixotic Scriptures,* D. W. Cruickshanks's "'Literature' and the Book Trade in Golden Age Spain," and Noël Salomon's "Algunos problemas de sociología de las literaturas de lengua española."

10. See Geoffrey Ribbans ("Meaning and Structure") for a complementary explanation of this scene, in which the progressive attitude of the villagers is contrasted with that of the supposedly more enlightened representatives of the cities.

11. Teresa Kirschner's study, *El protagonista colectivo en Fuenteovejuna de Lope de Vega,* offers a lucid examination of the relationship between speech and silence in the play, especially in the torture scene.

12. See Antonio Gómez Moriana *(Derecho de resistencia)* for a moral/ethical comparison between the actions of the villagers of Fuenteovejuna and the writings of St. Thomas Aquinas and Aristotle.

13. Ribbans observes:

Some critics have pointed out that such a revolt in the name of the king was actually legal in the fifteenth century. This is not strictly relevant to the play; Lope was not concerned with the fifteenth century, but with permanent social problems as he saw them mirrored in the seventeenth. Particularly, he is at pains to emphasize what an unmitigated social evil revolt is. ("Meaning and Structure" 167)

14. Francisco Ruiz Ramón concludes that Fuenteovejuna's heroism saves the town (*Historia* 159); Gerald Gillespie observes, "*Fuenteovejuna* is therefore a celebration of the triumph of justice; it is in its own times and circumstances a play about the establishment of valid authority" ("The Rebel" 331).

15. Teresa Kirschner observes:

> Se puede notar cómo el discurso de Flores está teñido por una visión que busca la completa exoneración del Comendador y la condena de los campesinos. Aunque en los detalles Flores no miente, se salta por encima precisamente los dos elementos que Lope ha elaborado con tanto cuidado para justificar el comportamiento de su protagonista: la enormidad de los abusos del Comendador y la fuerte adhesión de los campesinos al ideal de justicia de la monarquía.

[One can note how Flores's discourse is biased: he tries to exonerate the Comendador and condemn the peasants. Although Flores does not lie in his account of the details, he overlooks precisely the two elements Lope so carefully elaborated upon in his justification of the protagonist: on one hand the enormity of the Comendador's abuses, and on the other the peasants' strong adherence to the ideal of justice represented by the monarchy.]

(*El protagonista* 129)

16. See Josué Harari: 'Derridean deconstruction . . . consists more of the tracing of a path among textual strata in order to stir up and expose forgotten and dormant sediments of meaning which have accumulated and settled into the text's fabric" (37). See also Paul Julian Smith's *Writing in the Margin* for a related discussion of *Peribáñez* (esp. pp. 134–44).

Chapter 7. Literary History, Literary Theory, and *Cada uno para sí:* The Dramatist as Reader and Rewriter of His Own Text

1. Ruano concludes:

the adapter's main aim was to produce a version of the play suitable for performance before a rural audience. To this end, he paid scant attention to the historical background or to the literary and classical references, and expurgated the text of sexual allusions and socially unacceptable ideas. At the same time, he simplified themes, clarified ambiguous scenes, reiterated key images and symbols, emphasized important motifs, and stereotyped the main characters. In so doing, he gave us a unique and invaluable insight into how a seventheenth-century professional spectator understood Lope's complex and subtle play.

His task, however, did not end there. As a professional of the theater, the adapter was able to introduce some improvements in those areas of stagecraft with which he was best acquainted; namely, the staging of the play and the development and structure of the plot. . . . Thus, his rehash of *Peribáñez* results in a text which, although both poetically and linguistically vastly inferior to Lope's masterpiece, may be said to surpass its ancestor in some respects. ("An Early Rehash" 26–27)

2. See Martin Franzbach, *El teatro de Calderón en Europa* and Henry Sullivan, *Calderón in the German Lands and the Low Countries.*

3. The original composition of *Cada uno* was fixed by Hilborn as occurring in 1652 because of the play's historical reference to the fall of Barcelona. Ruano argues that the play can only be positively dated within the time period 1652–1661.

4. Unless otherwise indicated, all references to Ruano in the text derive from the introduction to his edition of *Cada uno para sí,* which incorporates the material found in the articles cited in the bibliography.

5. Jauss's ideas have been applauded by Paul de Man, who discussed Jauss in *Blindness and Insight* and who wrote the introduction to Jauss's *Toward an Aesthetic of Reception.* The relationship between history, collaboration, and guilt has been appropriated by de Man as a kind of literary (fictional) experience (see *Allegories of Reading*), which is clearly resonant of Jauss's philosophy (see also Jon Weiner's "Deconstructing de Man").

Bibliography

Amante, David J. "Ironic Language: A Structuralist Approach." *Language and Style* 13 (1980): 15–25.

Aníbal, Claude E. "The Historical Elements of Lope de Vega's *Fuente Ovejuna*." *PMLA* 49 (1934): 657–718.

Atkins, Douglas. *Reading Deconstruction.* Lexington: University of Kentucky Press, 1983.

Atkins, Douglas, and Laura Morrow, eds. *Contemporary Literary Theory.* Amherst: University of Massachusetts Press, 1989.

Auerbach, Nina. *Woman and the Demon.* Cambridge: Harvard University Press, 1982.

Austin, John L. *How to Do Things with Words.* Edited by J. O. Urmson and Marina Sbisà. 2d ed. Cambridge: Harvard University Press, 1975.

———. *Philosophical Papers.* London: Oxford University Press, 1961.

———. *Sense and Sensibilia.* London: Oxford University Press, 1962.

Bach, Kent, and Robert M. Harnish. *Linguistic Communication and Speech Acts.* Cambridge: MIT Press, 1982.

Benveniste, Emile. *Problems in General Linguistics.* Translated by M. E. Meek. Coral Gables: Miami University Press, 1971.

Bloom, Harold. *The Anxiety of Influence: A Theory of Poetry.* London: Oxford University Press, 1973.

Blue, William R. *The Development of Imagery in Calderón's Comedias.* York, S.C.: Spanish Literature Publications, 1983.

Brown, Robert L., and Martin Steinmann. "Native Readers of Fiction: A Genre Rule and Speech-Act Approach to Defining Literature." In *What is Literature?*, edited by Paul Hernadi, 141–60. Bloomington: Indiana University Press, 1978.

Brushwood, John S. *Genteel Barbarism: New Readings of Nineteenth-Century Spanish American Novels.* Lincoln: Nebraska University Press, 1981.

Bullough, Edward. " 'Psychical Distance' and a Factor in Art and an Esthetic Principle." In *A Modern Book of Esthetics,* edited by Melvin Rader. 3d. ed., 394–411. N.p.: Holt, 1960.

Burns, Elizabeth. *Theatricality: A Study of Convention in the Theatre and in Social Life.* New York: Harper and Row, 1972.

Burton, Deirdre. *Dialogue and Discourse.* London: Routledge and Kegan Paul, 1980.

———. "Conversation Pieces." In *Literary Text and Language Study,* edited by Ronald Carter and D. Burton. London: Edward Arnold, 1982.

Cain, William. "Reply to Lentricchia's 'On Behalf of Theory.' " In *Criticism in the*

University, edited by Gerald Graff and Reginald Gibbons. Evanston, Ill.: Northwestern University Press, 1985.

Calderón de la Barca, Pedro. *Cada uno para sí.* Edited by José Ruano de la Haza. Kassel: Reichenberger, 1982.

———. *Cada uno para sí.* MS.16,887. Madrid: Biblioteca Nacional.

———. *La dama duende.* Edited by Angel Valbuena Briones. 6th ed. Madrid: Cátedra, 1984.

———. *En la vida todo es verdad y todo mentira.* Edited by D. W. Cruickshank. London: Tamesis, 1971.

———. *Quarta parte de Comedias,* vol. 10. Edited by D. W. Cruickshank and J. E. Varey. Westmead and London: Gregg and Tamesis Books, 1973.

Cameron, Deborah. *Feminism and Linguistic Theory.* New York: St. Martin's Press, 1985.

Casa, Frank. "The Dramatic Unity of *El caballero de Olmedo.*" *Neophilologus* 50 (1966): 234–43.

Casa, Frank, and Michael McGaha, eds. *Editing the Comedia.* Ann Arbor: Michigan Romance Studies (vol. 5), 1985.

Cascardi, Anthony J. *The Limits of Illusion: A Critical Study of Calderón.* Cambridge: Cambridge University Press, 1984.

Castro, Américo. *"El caballero de Olmedo."* In *Essays on Hispanic Literature in Honor of Edmund L. King,* edited by Silvia Molloy and Luis Fernández Cifuentes, 31–44. London: Tamesis Books, 1983.

Castro Leal, Antonio. *Juan Ruiz de Alarcón: su vida y su obra.* Mexico: Cuadernos Americanos, 1943.

Caton, Charles E., ed. *Philosophy and Ordinary Language.* Urbana: Illinois University Press, 1963.

Chatman, Seymour. *Story and Discourse.* Ithaca: Cornell University Press, 1978.

Chatman, Seymour, and Samuel R. Levin, eds. *Essays in the Language of Literature.* Boston: Houghton Mifflin, 1967.

Cohen, Walter. *Drama of a Nation: Public Theater in Renaissance England and Spain.* Ithaca: Cornell University Press, 1985.

Cooper, Marilyn M. "Implicatures in Fictional Conversations from *Days of Our Lives* and *Mary Hartman, Mary Hartman.*" *Centrum* 5 (1977): 5–19.

Correas, Gonzalo. *Vocabulario de refranes.* 2d ed. Madrid: Revista de Archivos, 1924.

Cotarelo y Mori, Emilio. *Don Francisco de Rojas Zorrilla.* Madrid: Revista de Archivos, 1911.

Cruickshank, D. W. "Calderón's Handwriting." *Modern Language Review* 65 (1970): 65–77.

———. "The Editing of Spanish Golden-Age Plays from Early Printed Versions." In *Editing the Comedia,* edited by Frank Casa and Michael McGaha, 52–103. Ann Arbor: Michigan Romance Studies (vol. 5), 1985.

———. "'Literature' and the Book Trade in Golden-Age Spain." *Modern Language Review* 73 (1978): 799–824.

Culler, Jonathan. "Convention and Meaning: Derrida and Austin." *New Literary History* 13 (1981): 15–30.

———. *On Deconstruction: Theory and Criticism After Structuralism.* Ithaca: Cornell University Press, 1982.

———. *The Pursuit of Signs: Semiotics, Literature, Deconstruction.* Ithaca: Cornell University Press, 1981.

Darst, David. "Hidden Truths and Wrong Assumptions in *La verdad sospechosa.*" *Revista de estudios hispánicos* 13 (1979): 439–47.

De Armas, Frederick. *The Invisible Mistress: Aspects of Feminism and Fantasy in the Golden Age.* Charlottesville: Biblioteca Siglo de Oro, 1976.

De Man, Paul. *Allegories of Reading: Figural Language in Rousseau, Nietzsche, Rilke, and Proust.* New Haven: Yale University Press, 1979.

———. *Blindness and Insight: Essays in the Rhetoric of Contemporary Criticism.* New York: Oxford University Press, 1971.

———. *The Resistance to Theory.* Minneapolis: University of Minnesota Press, 1986.

———. "Semiology and Rhetoric." In *Textual Strategies,* edited by Josué V. Harari, 121–40. Ithaca, N.Y.: Cornell University Press, 1979.

Derrida, Jacques. *Of Grammatology.* Translated by Gayatri C. Spivak. Baltimore: Johns Hopkins University Press, 1974.

———. "Limited Inc abc. . . ." *Glyph* 2 (1977): 162–254.

———. *Positions.* Translated by Alan Bass. Chicago: University of Chicago Press, 1981.

———. "Signature Event Context." *Glyph* 1 (1977): 172–97.

———. *Writing and Difference.* Translated by Alan Bass. Chicago: University of Chicago Press, 1978.

DiLillo, Leonard M. "Moral Purpose in Ruiz de Alarcón's *La verdad sospechosa.*" *Hispania* 56 (1973): 254–59.

Dodd, William M. "Conversation, Dialogue, and Exposition." *Strumenti Critici* 15 (1981): 171–91.

Durán, Manuel. "Lope y el teatro de acción." *Hispanófila* 18 (1963): 3–14.

Eagleton, Terry. *Literary Theory: An Introduction.* Minneapolis: Minnesota University Press, 1983.

Elam, Keir. "Language in the Theater." *Sub-stance* 18 (1977): 139–61.

———. *The Semiotics of Theatre and Drama.* London: Methuen, 1980.

———. *Shakespeare's Universe of Discourse: Language-Games in the Comedies.* Cambridge: Cambridge University Press, 1984.

Ellis, John M. "What Does Deconstruction Contribute to Theory of Criticism?" *New Literary History* 19 (1988): 259–79.

Fann, K. T., ed. *Symposium on J. L. Austin.* London: Allen and Union, 1969.

Felman, Shoshana. *The Literary Speech Act: Don Juan with J. L. Austin, or Seduction in Two Languages.* Translated by Catherine Porter. Ithaca, N.Y.: Cornell University Press, 1983.

Fiore, Robert L. "The Interaction of Motives and Mores in *La verdad sospechosa.*" *Hispanófila* 61 (1977): 513–27.

Fischer, Susan L. "The Invisible Partner: A Jungian Approach to Calderón's *La dama duende.*" *Revista canadiense de estudios hispánicos* 7 (1983): 231–47.

Fish, Stanley. "Consequences." *Critical Inquiry* 11 (1985): 433–58.

———. "How To Do Things with Austin and Searle: Speech-Act Theory and Literary Criticism." In *Is There a Text in This Class?*, 197–245. Cambridge: Harvard University Press, 1980.

———. "With the Compliments of the Author: Reflections on Derrida and Austin." *Critical Inquiry* 8 (1982): 693–721.

Flew, Antony, ed. *Essays in Conceptual Analysis.* London: MacMillan, 1960.

Franzbach, Martin. *El teatro de Calderón en Europa.* Madrid: Fundación Universitaria Española, 1982.

Fothergill-Payne, Louise. "La justicia poética de *La verdad sospechosa.*" *Romanische Forchungen* 83 (1971): 588–95.

Foucault, Michel. *The Order of Things: An Archaeology of the Human Sciences.* (Originally published as *Les mots et les choses.*) New York: Vintage Books, 1973.

Friedman, Edward H. " 'Girl Gets Boy': A Note on the Value of Exchange in the *Comedia.*" *Bulletin of the Comediantes* 39 (1987): 75–84.

Gann, Myra S. "The Performative Status of Verbal Offenses in *A secreto agravio, secreta venganza.*" In *Things Done with Words,* edited by Elias L. Rivers, 39–49. Newark, Del.: Juan de la Cuesta, 1986.

Gérard, A. S. "Baroque Unity and the Dualities of *El caballero de Olmedo.*" *Romanic Review* 56 (1965): 92–106.

Gilbert, Sandra. "What Do Feminist Critics Want? A Postcard from the Volcano." In *The New Feminist Literary Criticism: Essays on Women, Literature, and Theory,* edited by Elaine Showalter, 29–45. New York: Pantheon, 1985.

Gilbert, Sandra, and Susan Gubar. *The Madwoman in the Attic: The Woman Writer and the Nineteenth-Century Literary Imagination.* New Haven, Conn.: Yale University Press, 1984.

Gillespie, Gerald. "The Rebel in Seventeenth-Century Tragedy." *Comparative Literature* 18 (1966): 324–36.

Glannon, Walter. "What Literary Theory Misses in Wittgenstein." *Philosophy and Literature* 10 (1986): 263–72.

Gómez-Moriana, Antonio. *Derecho de resistencia y tiranicidio. Estudio de una temática en las "Comedias" de Lope de Vega.* Santiago de Compostela: Porto, 1968.

Goodheart, Eugene. "The Text and the Interpretive Community." *Daedalus* 112 (1983): 215–31.

Gouldson, Kathleen. "Three Studies in Golden Age Drama." In *Spanish Golden Age Poetry and Drama,* edited by Allison Peers, 63–118. Liverpool: Institute of Hispanic Studies, 1946.

Greene, Gayle, and Coppélia Kahn, eds. *Making a Difference: Feminist Literary Criticism.* London: Methuen, 1985.

Greer, Margaret Rich. "Calderón, Copyists, and the Problem of Endings." *Bulletin of the Comediantes* 36 (1984): 71–81.

Grice, H. Paul. "Logic and Conversation." In *Syntax and Semantics. Vol. III: Speech Acts,* edited by Peter Cole and Jerry L. Morgan, 41–58. New York: Academic Press, 1975.

Gurza, Esperanza. "Speech Act Theory Applied." *Confluencia: Revista Hispánica de Cultura y Literatura* 1 (1986): 85–97.

Hallett, Garth. *A Companion to Wittgenstein's "Philosophical Investigations."* Ithaca: Cornell University Press, 1977.

Hancher, Michael. "Beyond a Speech-Act Theory of Literary Discourse." *MLN* 92 (1977): 1081–98.

———. "The Classification of Cooperative Illocutionary Acts." *Language and Society* 8 (1979): 1–14.

———. "What Kind of Speech Act Is Interpretation?" *Poetics* 10 (1981): 263–82.

Harari, Josué V. "Critical Factions/Critical Fictions." In *Textual Strategies: Perspectives in Post-Structuralist Criticism,* edited by J. V. Harari, 17–72. Ithaca, N.Y.: Cornell University Press, 1979.

Hartman, Geoffrey. "Criticism, Indeterminacy, Irony." In *What is Criticism?,* edited by Paul Hernadi, 113–25. Bloomington: Indiana University Press, 1981.

———. *Criticism in the Wilderness: The Study of Literature Today.* New Haven: Yale University Press, 1980.

Hicks, Margaret R. "Strategies of Ambiguity: The Honor Conflict in *La batalla de honor.*" In *Things Done with Words,* edited by Elias L. Rivers, 15–27. Newark, Del.: Juan de la Cuesta, 1986.

High, Dallas M. *Language, Persons, and Belief: Studies in Wittgenstein's Philosophical Investigations and Religious Uses of Language.* New York: Oxford University Press, 1967.

Hilborn, H. W. *Chronology of the Plays of D. Pedro Calderón de la Barca.* Toronto: Toronto University Press, 1938.

Holloway, James E. "Lope's Neoplatonism: *La dama boba.*" *Bulletin of Hispanic Studies* 49 (1972): 236–55.

Honig, Edwin. *Calderón and the Seizures of Honor.* Cambridge: Harvard University Press, 1972.

Hornby, Richard. *Drama, Metadrama, and Perception.* Lewisburg: Bucknell University Press, 1986.

Hoy, David C. *The Critical Circle: Literary History and Philosophical Hermeneutics.* Berkeley: California University Press, 1978.

Hunter, William F. "Editing Texts in Multiple Versions." In *Editing the Comedia,* edited by Frank P. Casa and Michael McGaha, 24–51. Ann Arbor: Michigan Romance Studies (vol. 5), 1985.

Hutchinson, Chris. "The Act of Narration: A Critical Survey of Some Speech-Act Theories of Narrative Discourse." *Journal of Literary Semantics* 13 (1984): 3–34.

Ingarden, Roman. "The Functions of Language in the Theater." In *The Literary Work of Art,* translated by G. Grabowicz, 377–96. Evanston, Ill.: Northwestern Univ. Press, 1973.

Iser, Wolfgang. *The Act of Reading: A Theory of Aesthetic Response.* Baltimore: Johns Hopkins University Press, 1978.

Jakobson, Roman. "Linguistics and Poetics." In *Essays on the Language of Literature,* edited by Seymour Chatman and Samuel R. Levin, 296–322. Boston: Houghton Mifflin, 1967.

Jauss, Hans Robert. *Aesthetic Reception and Literary Hermeneutics.* Translated by Michael Shaw. Minneapolis: Minneapolis University Press, 1982.

———. "The Identity of the Poetic Text in the Changing Horizon of Understanding." In *Identity of the Literary Text,* edited by Mario J. Valdés and Owen Miller, 146–74. Toronto: Toronto University Press, 1985.

———. "Literary History as a Challenge to Literary Theory." *New Literary History* 2 (1970): 7–37. Revised in *Toward an Aesthetic of Reception.*

———. *Toward an Aesthetic of Reception.* Translated by Timothy Bahti. Minneapolis: Minnesota University Press, 1982.

Johnson, Barbara. *The Critical Difference: Essays in the Contemporary Rhetoric of Reading.* Baltimore: Johns Hopkins University Press, 1980.

King, Willard F., intro. *The Knight of Olmedo.* Lincoln: Nebraska University Press, 1972.

Kirschner, Teresa. *El protagonista colectivo en Fuenteovejuna de Lope de Vega.* Salamanca: Salamanca University Press, 1979.

Knapp, Steven, and Walter Benn Michaels. "Against Theory." *Critical Inquiry* 8 (1982): 723–42.

Kowzan, Tadeusz. "Art 'en abyme.'" *Diogenes* 96 (1976): 67–92.

———. "El signo en el teatro." In *El teatro y su crisis actual,* edited by Theodor W. Adorno, et al., 25–51. Caracas: Monte Avila, 1969.

Kripke, Saul. *Naming and Necessity.* Cambridge: Harvard University Press, 1972.

Kristeva, Julia. *The Kristeva Reader.* Edited by Toril Moi. New York: Columbia University Press, 1986.

Larson, Catherine. "Labels and Lies: Names and Don García's World in *La verdad sospechosa.*" *Revista de estudios hispánicos* 20 (1986): 95–112.

———. "*La dama duende* and the Shifting Characterization of Calderón's Diabolical Angel." In *The Presence of Women in Spanish Golden Age Drama,* edited by D. L. Smith and A. K. Stoll, 33–50. Lewisburg: Bucknell University Press, 1991.

———. "Speech Act Theory and Linguistic Approaches to Teaching the *Comedia.*" In *Approaches to Teaching Spanish Golden Age Drama,* edited by Everett W. Hesse, 43–55. York, S.C.: Spanish Literature Publications, 1988.

———. "Test-Driving the *Comedia*: Transmission, Filters, and Brakes." In *Texto y espectáculo: Nuevas dimensiones críticas de la comedia,* edited by Arturo Pérez-Pisonero, 73–79. New Brunswick, N.J.: SLUSA, 1990.

———. "'Yo quiero hablar claro': Language as the Motivating Force of Lope's *La dama boba.*" In *Things Done with Words,* edited by Elias Rivers, 29–38. Newark, Del.: Juan de la Cuesta, 1986.

Larson, Donald R. "*La dama boba* and the Comic Sense of Life." *Romanische Forschungen* 85 (1973): 41–62.

Leech, Geoffrey N. *Principles of Pragmatics.* London: Longman, 1983.

Leiber, Justin. "How J. L. Austin Does Things with Words." *Philosophy and Literature* 1 (1976): 54–65.

Leitch, Vincent B. *Deconstructive Criticism.* New York: Columbia University Press, 1983.

Lihani, John. "A Literary Jargon of Early Spanish Drama: The Sayagués Dialect." In *Linguistic Approaches to the Romance Lexicon.* edited by Frank H. Nuesrel, Jr., 39–44. Washington, D.C.: Georgetown University Press, 1978.

Loftis, John. *The Spanish Plays of Neoclassical England.* New Haven: Yale University Press, 1973.

Lyons, John D. "Discourse and Authority in *Le Menteur.*" In *Corneille comique,* edited by Milorad R. Margitic, 151–68. N.p.: Papers on French 17th Century Literature/Biblio 17, 1982.

MacCurdy, Raymond, ed. *Spanish Drama of the Golden Age*. New York: Appleton-Century-Crofts, 1971.

———. "Women and Sexual Love in the Plays of Rojas Zorrilla: Tradition and Innovation." *Hispania* 62 (1979): 255–65.

———. *Francisco de Rojas Zorrilla*. New York: Twayne, 1968.

———. *Francisco de Rojas Zorrilla: Bibliografía crítica*. Madrid: CSIC, 1965.

Margitic, Milorad R. "Le discours direct comme forme verbale d'illusion théâtrale chez Corneille." *Kentucky Romance Quarterly* 23 (1976): 513–27.

Margolis, Joseph. "Literature and Speech Acts." *Philosophy and Literature* 3 (1979): 39–52.

Marín, Juan María, ed. and intro. *Fuente Ovejuna*. 8th ed. Madrid: Cátedra, 1987.

Maldonado, Felipe C., ed. *Refanero clásico español y otros dichos populares*. Madrid: Taurus, 1960.

Marlow, James, and William Powers. "Fish Doing Things with Austin and Searle." *MLN* 91 (1976): 1603–24.

McCrary, William C. *The Goldfinch and the Hawk: A Study of Lope de Vega's Tragedy El caballero de Olmedo*. Chapel Hill: North Carolina University Press, 1966.

———. "*Fuenteovejuna*: Its Platonic Vision and Execution." *Studies in Philology* 58 (1961): 179–92.

McDonald, W. Brock. "How to Catch Fish With Words." *Texte* 3 (1984): 29–41.

McKendrick, Melveena. "Language and Silence in *El castigo sin venganza*." *Bulletin of the Comediantes* 35 (1983): 79–95.

———. *Woman and Society in the Spanish Drama of the Golden Age*. London: Cambridge University Press, 1974.

Menéndez y Pelayo, Marcelino. *Estudios sobre el teatro de Lope de Vega*, vol. 5. Edited by Enrique Sánchez Reyes. Santander: Aldus, 1949.

Miller, J. Hillis. "Stevens' Rock and Criticism as Cure, II." *Georgia Review* 30 (1976): 330–48.

Moi, Toril. *Sexual/Textual Politics*. London: Methuen, 1985.

Moir, Duncan W. "Lope de Vega's *Fuenteovejuna* and the *Emblemas morales* of Sebastián de Covarrubias Horozco." In *Homenaje a William Fichter*, edited by A. David Kossoff and José Amor y Vásquez, 537–46. Madrid: Castalia, 1971.

Morton, John G. "Alarcón's *La verdad sospechosa:* Meaning and Didacticism." *Bulletin of the Comediantes* 26 (1974): 51–57.

Norrick, Neal R. "Nondirect Speech Acts and Double Binds." *Poetics* 10 (1980): 33–47.

Ohmann, Richard. "Speech Acts and the Definition of Literature." *Philosophy and Rhetoric* 4 (1971): 1–19.

———. "Speech, Literature, and the Space Between." *New Literary History* 4 (1972): 47–63.

Parker, Alexander A. *The Approach to the Spanish Drama of the Golden Age. Diamante* 6. London: Hispanic and Luso-Brazilian Council, 1957. Rpt. in *Tulane Drama Review* 4 (1959): 42–59. Revised as "The Spanish Drama of the Golden Age: Method of Analysis and Interpretation." In *The Great Playwrights*, edited by Eric Bentley, 679–707. Garden City, N.Y.: Doubleday, 1970.

———. "Reflections of a New Definition of Baroque Drama." *Bulletin of Hispanic Studies* 30 (1953): 142–51.

Parker, Patricia, and Geoffrey Hartman, eds. *Shakespeare and the Question of Theory.* New York: Methuen, 1985.

Parker, Patricia, and David Quint, eds. *Literary Theory/Renaissance Texts.* Baltimore: Johns Hopkins University Press, 1986.

Parr, James A. "An Essay on Critical Method, Applied to the *Comedia.*" *Hispania* 57 (1974): 434–44.

———. "Honor-Virtue in *La verdad sospechosa* and *Las paredes oyen.*" *Revista de estudios hispánicos* 8 (1974): 173–88.

Paterson, Alan K. "Reversal and Multiple Role-Playing in Alarcón's *La verdad sospechosa.*" *Bulletin of Hispanic Studies* 61 (1984): 361–68.

Pavis, Patrice. *Languages of the Stage: Essays in the Semiology of Theatre.* New York: Performing Arts Journal Publications, 1982.

Petrey, Sandy. "Speech Acts in Society: Fish, Felman, Austin, and God." *Texte* 3 (1984): 43–61.

Place, Edwin B. "Notes on the Grotesque: The *Comedia de figurón* at Home and Abroad." *PMLA* 54 (1939): 412–21.

Poesse, Walter. *Juan Ruiz de Alarcón.* New York: Twayne, 1972.

Porter, Joseph. *The Drama of Speech Acts.* Berkeley: California University Press, 1979.

Pratt, Mary Louise. "The Ideology of Speech-Act Theory." *Centrum* 1 (1981): 5–18.

———. *Toward a Speech Act Theory of Literary Discourse.* Bloomington: Indiana University Press, 1977.

Pratt, Mary Louise, and Elizabeth Closs Traugott. *Linguistics for Students of Literature.* New York: Harcourt Brace Jovanovich, 1980.

Quigley, Austin E. "Wittgenstein's Philosophizing and Literary Theorizing." *New Literary History* 19 (1988): 209–37.

Rades y Andrada, Francisco de. *Chronica de las tres Ordenes y Cauallerias de Santiago, Calatraua y Alcantara.* Toledo: Juan de Ayala, 1572.

Ramírez Arellano, Rafael. "Rebelión de Fuente Obejuna contra el Comendador Mayor de Calatrava Fernán Gómez de Guzmán (1476)." *Boletín de la Real Academia de la Historia* 39 (1901): 446–512.

Read, Malcolm K. *The Birth and Death of Language: Spanish Literature and Linguistics: 1300–1700.* Madrid: Porrúa, 1983.

Reichenberger, Arnold G. "Editing Spanish *Comedias* of the XVIIth Century: History and Present-Day Practice." In *Editing the Comedia,* edited by Frank P. Casa and Michael McGaha, 1–23. Ann Arbor: Michigan Romance Studies (vol. 5), 1985.

Ribbans, Geoffrey. "Lying in the Structure of *La verdad sospechosa.*" In *Studies in Spanish Literature of the Golden Age Presented to Edward M. Wilson,* edited by R. O. Jones, 193–216. London: Tamesis Books, 1973.

———. "The Meaning and Structure of Lope's *Fuenteovejuna.*" *Bulletin of Hispanic Studies* 31 (1954): 150–70.

Rich, Adrienne. "Planetarium." *Poems, Selected and New, 1950–1974.* New York: Norton, 1975.

Rifelj, Carol de Dobay. "Deconstruction Workers: Philosophy and Literature." Unpublished ms.

Riley, E. C. "Alarcón's *mentiroso* in the Light of the Contemporary Theory of Character." In *Critical Essays on the Life and Work of Juan Ruiz de Alarcón,* edited by James A. Parr, 225–36. Madrid: Dos Continentes, 1972.

Rivers, Elias L. *Quixotic Scriptures: Essays on the Textuality of Hispanic Literature.* Bloomington: Indiana University Press, 1983.

———. "The Shame of Writing in *La Estrella de Sevilla.*" *Folio* 2 (1980): 105–17.

———. "Written Poetry and Oral Speech Acts in Calderón's Plays." *Aureum Saeculum Hispanum* (1983): 271–84.

———, ed. *Things Done with Words: Speech Acts in Hispanic Drama.* Newark, Del.: Juan de la Cuesta, 1986.

Rojas Zorrilla, Francisco de. *Entre bobos anda el juego.* In *Spanish Drama of the Golden Age,* edited by Raymond MacCurdy, 521–72. New York: Appleton-Century-Crofts, 1971.

———. *Entre bobos anda el juego.* Edited by Juan Loveluck. Santiago, Chile: Zig-Zag, 1957.

———. *Entre bobos anda el juego.* Edited by Agustín del Saz. Madrid: CIAP, 1929.

Ruano de la Haza, José. "An Early Rehash of Lope's *Peribáñez.*" *Bulletin of the Comediantes* 35 (1983): 5–29.

———. "La edición crítica de *Cada uno para sí.*" In *Hacia Calderón,* 126–47. Berlin: Walter de Gruyter, 1976.

———. "Estructura e interpretación en una comedia de capa y espada de Calderón: *Cada uno para sí.*" In *Hacia Calderón,* 106–16. Berlin: Walter de Gruyter, 1979.

———. "Two Seventeenth-Century Scribes of Calderón." *Modern Language Review* 73 (1978): 71–81.

Ruiz de Alarcón, Juan. *La verdad sospechosa.* In *Diez Comedias del Siglo de Oro,* edited by José Martel and Hymen Alpern. 2d. ed., 517–604. New York: Harper and Row, 1968.

———. *La verdad sospechosa,* vol. 2 of *Obras completas de Juan Ruiz de Alarcón.* Edited by Agustín Millares Carlo. (Mexico: Fondo de Cultura Económica, 1959), 363–470.

Ruiz Ramón, Francisco. *Historia del teatro español: Desde sus orígenes hasta 1900.* 3d. ed. Madrid: Cátedra, 1979.

Ruthven, K. K. *Feminist Literary Studies.* Cambridge: Cambridge University Press, 1984.

Sage, J. W. *Lope de Vega: El caballero de Olmedo.* London: Grant and Cutler, 1974.

Salomon, Noël. "Algunos problemas de sociología de las literaturas de lengua española." In *Creación y público en la literatura española,* edited by J.-F. Botrel and S. Salaün, 15–39. Madrid: Castalia, 1974.

Saussure, Ferdinand de. *Course in General Linguistics.* Edited by Charles Bally, et al. Translated by Wade Baskin. New York: McGraw-Hill, 1959.

Savona, Jeanette Laillou. "*Didascalies* as Speech Act." Translated by Fiona Strachan. *Modern Drama* 25 (1982): 25–35.

Schizzano Mandel, Adrienne. "La *dama* juega el *duende*: Pretexto, geno-texto y feno-texto." *Bulletin of the Comediantes* 37 (1985): 41–54.

Searle, John R. *Expression and Meaning: Studies in the Theory of Speech Acts.* Cambridge: Cambridge University Press, 1979.

———. "The Logical Status of Fictional Discourse." *New Literary History* 5 (1975): 319–32.

———. "Proper Names." *Mind* 67 (1958): 166–73.

———. "Reiterating the Differences: A Reply to Derrida." *Glyph* 1 (1977): 198–208.

———. *Speech Acts: An Essay in the Philosophy of Language.* London: Cambridge University Press, 1969.

———. "What is a Speech Act?" In *Language and Social Context,* edited by Pier Paolo Giglioli, 136–74. London: Penguin, 1972.

———. "The Word Turned Upside Down." *New York Review of Books.* 27 October 1983: 74–79.

Selden, Raman. *A Reader's Guide to Contemporary Literary Theory.* Lexington: University of Kentucky Press, 1985.

Seung, T. K. *Semiotics and Thematics in Hermeneutics.* New York: Columbia University Press, 1982.

Short, M. H. "Discourse Analysis and the Analysis of Drama." *Applied Linguistics* 2 (1981): 180–202.

Showalter, Elaine. "Toward a Feminist Poetics." In *The New Feminist Criticism: Essays on Women, Literature, and Theory,* edited by Elaine Showalter, 125–43. New York: Pantheon, 1985.

Sloman, Albert E. "The Phonology of Moorish Jargon in Two Works of Early Spanish Dramatists and Lope de Vega." *Modern Language Review* 44 (1949): 207–17.

Smith, Barbara Herrnstein. *On the Margins of Discourse: The Relation of Literature to Language.* Chicago: University of Chicago Press, 1978.

Smith, Paul Julian. *Writing in the Margin: Spanish Literature of the Golden Age.* Oxford: Clarendon Press, 1988.

Soons, Alan. "*La verdad sospechosa* in its Epoch." In *Critical Essays on the Life and Work of Juan Ruiz de Alarcón,* edited by James A. Parr, 239–45. Madrid: Dos Continentes, 1972.

———. "Towards an Interpretation of *El caballero de Olmedo.*" *Romanische Forschungen* 73 (1961): 160–68.

Spitzer, Leo. "A Central Theme and its Structural Equivalent in Lope's *Fuenteovejuna.*" *Hispanic Review* 23 (1955): 274–92.

———. *Linguistics and Literary History.* Princeton: Princeton University Press, 1948.

Spivak, Gayatri. "Revolutions That as Yet Have No Model: Derrida's *Limited Inc.*" *Diacritics* 10 (1980): 29–49.

Staten, Henry. "Wittgenstein's Boundaries." *New Literary History* 19 (1988): 309–18.

Stern, Charlotte. "Dulcinea, Aldonza, and the Theory of Speech Acts." *Hispania* 67 (1984): 61–73.

Strawson, P. F. "On Referring." In *Essays in Conceptual Analysis,* edited by Antony Flew, 21–52. London: Macmillan, 1956.

Stroud, Matthew D. "Social-Comic Anagnorisis in *La dama duende.*" *Bulletin of the Comediantes* 29 (1977): 96–102.

Sullivan, Henry W. *Calderón in the German Lands and the Low Countries: His Reception and Influence, 1654–1980.* Cambridge: Cambridge University Press, 1983.

Sunderman, Paula. "Speech Act Theory and Faulkner's 'That Evening Sun.'" *Language and Style* 14 (1981): 304–14.

Surtz, Ronald. "Daughter of Night, Daughter of Light: The Imagery of Finea's Transformation in *La dama boba.*" *Bulletin of the Comediantes* 13 (1961): 161–67.

ter Horst, Robert. *Calderón: The Secular Plays.* Lexington: University of Kentucky Press, 1982.

———. "The True Mind of Marriage: Ironies of the Intellect in Lope's *La dama boba.*" *Romanistiches Jahrbuch* 27 (1976): 347–63.

———. "The Ruling Temper of Calderón's *La dama duende.*" *Bulletin of the Comediantes* 27 (1975): 68–72.

Turner, Alison. "The Dramatic Function of Imagery and Symbolism in *Peribáñez* and *El caballero de Olmedo.*" *Symposium* 20 (1966): 174–86.

Valbuena-Briones, Angel. "Los papeles cómicos y las hablas dialectales en dos comedias de Calderón." *De thesaurus, Boletín del Instituto Caro y Cuervo* 42 (1987): 1–13.

Valbuena Prat, Angel. *Literatura dramática española.* Barcelona: Labor, 1950.

Valdés. Mario J., and Owen Miller. *Identity of the Literary Text.* Toronto: Toronto University Press, 1985.

Varey, John E. "Staging and Stage Directions." In *Editing the Comedia,* edited by Frank Casa and Michael McGaha, 146–61. Ann Arbor: Michigan Romance Studies (vol. 5), 1985.

Vega Carpio, Lope de. *El caballero de Olmedo.* Edited by Francisco Rico. 6th ed. Madrid: Cátedra, 1985.

———. *La dama boba.* Edited by Diego Marín. 5th ed. Madrid: Cátedra, 1981.

———. "To the Duke of Sessa," In *Lope de Vega y sus cartas, III,* edited by Agustín G. de Amezúa. Madrid: Artes Gráficas "Aldus," 1941.

———. *Fuente Ovejuna.* Edited by Juan María Marín. 8th ed. Madrid: Cátedra, 1987.

Wardropper, Bruce W. "An Apology for Philology." *Modern Language Notes* 102 (1987): 176–90.

———. "The Criticism of the Spanish *Comedia: El Caballero de Olmedo* as Object Lesson." *Philological Quarterly* 51.1 (1972): 177–96.

———. "*Fuente Ovejuna: El gusto* and *lo justo.*" *Studies in Philology* 53 (1956): 159–71.

———. "Lope's *La dama boba* and Baroque Comedy." *Bulletin of the Comediantes* 13 (1961): 1–3.

Weiner, Jon. "Deconstructing de Man." *The Nation* 9 (January 1988): 22–24.

Weisner, Merry E. "Women's Defense of Their Public Role." In *Women in the Middle Ages and the Renaissance,* edited by Mary Beth Rose, 1–27. Syracuse, N.Y.: Syracuse University Press, 1986.

Wilshire, Bruce. *Role Playing and Identity: The Limits of Theatre as Metaphor.* Bloomington: Indiana University Press, 1982.

Wilson, E. M. "Calderón and the Stage Censor in the Seventeenth Century: A Provisional Study." *Symposium* 15 (1961): 165–84.

Wittgenstein, Ludwig. *The Blue and Brown Books.* New York: Harper and Row, 1958.

———. *Philosophical Investigations.* Translated by G. E. M. Anscombe. Oxford: Basil Blackwell, 1953.

Woodmansee, Martha. "Speech Act Theory and the Perpetuation of the Dogma of Literary Antonomy." *Centrum* 6 (1978): 75–89.

Ziomek, Henryk. *A History of Spanish Golden Age Drama.* Lexington: University of Kentucky Press, 1984.

Index